Communicating With the Dead

Reach Beyond the Grave

Jeff Belanger,

author of The World's Most Haunted Places

New Page Books
A division of The Career Press, Inc.
Franklin Lakes, NJ

COMMUNICATING WITH THE DEAD

EDITED AND TYPESET BY CLAYTON W. LEADBETTER

Cover photo by Jim DeCaro

Cover design by Jean William Naumann

Printed in the U.S.A. by Book-mart Press

To order this title, please call toll-free 1-800-CAREER-1 (NJ and Canada: 201-848-0310) to order using VISA or MasterCard, or for further information on books from Career Press.

XVII The Star © Kris Waldherr Art and Words. Used by permission. All rights reserved. *www.artandwords.com.*

The Goddess Tarot published by US Games Systems, Inc., Stamford, CT. *www.usgamesinc.com.*

9 of Arrows © Kris Waldherr Art and Words. Used by permission. All rights reserved. *www.artandwords.com.*

The Lover's Path Tarot published by US Games Systems, Inc., Stamford, CT. *www.usgamesinc.com.*

The Shining Tribe Tarot, by Rachel Pollack © 2001 Llewellyn Worldwide, Ltd. PO Box 64383, St. Paul, MN 55164. All rights reserved, used by permission of the publisher.

The four photos provided by Mark Macy copyright © 2005 by Mark Macy. Reprinting by permission only.

The Career Press, Inc., 3 Tice Road, PO Box 687,
Franklin Lakes, NJ 07417
www.careerpress.com
www.newpagebooks.com

Library of Congress Cataloging-in-Publication Data

Belanger, Jeff.
  Communicating with the dead : reach beyond the grave / by Jeff Belanger.
    p. cm.
  Includes bibliographical references and index.
  ISBN 1-56414-793-2 (pbk.)
  1. Spiritualism. I. Title

BF1261.2.B45 2005
133.9'1--dc22   2005041544

For Mom and Dad, who bought me
my first Ouija board—
this is all your fault.
Thanks for being open-minded and
for pushing me to pursue my dreams.

Acknowledgments

I'm the first to admit that I don't have all of the answers. But I do have a lot of questions. In putting this book together, I consulted with scientists, clergy, psychics, skeptics, and people who incorporate spirit communication devices into their own spirituality. Each person I interviewed shared something with me, and I would like to sincerely thank everyone I spoke with for the trust they put in me to document their ideas, and in some cases, very personal experiences. I worked hard to live up to all of your expectations.

I'd like to thank my wife, Megan, who not only puts up with my work—which can be very much on the fringe at times— but who also puts up with me. She's my best critic, my best friend, and I couldn't do any of this without her.

A big thank-you to Michael Pye, who was willing to take a chance on me again. Thanks also to Linda Rienecker, Laurie Kelly-Pye, Ron Fry, and all of the great folks at New Page Books who have been so supportive. I'd especially like to thank my editor, Clayton Leadbetter, who cared deeply about this project and helped make this book better.

I'm blessed to have a circle of friends who I can bounce ideas off of, get feedback from, and who are always ready to help when asked. Thank you Lee Prosser, Darci Faiello, Jim DeCaro, Tamara Thorne, Chris Quirk, and the folks at the Enchanted Fox metaphysical shop in Medway, Massachusetts.

Finally, a big thank-you to the Ghostvillagers—the citizens of Ghostvillage.com. You're always ready to weigh in with your thoughts, offer support, and challenge us with new ideas, approaches, and techniques. You certainly make our world and the spirit world a more interesting place!

Contents

Introduction 9

Chapter 1: Talking Boards 13

Chapter 2: Tarot Cards 37

Chapter 3: Spirit Photography 61

Chapter 4: Thomas Edison's
   Lost Spirit Communication Apparatus 91

Chapter 5: Electronic Voice Phenomena 107

Chapter 6: Instrumental Transcommunication 129

Chapter 7: Runes 149

Chapter 8: Mirror Gazing 165

Chapter 9: Dowsing 185

Chapter 10: Automatic Writing 213

Conclusion 237

Bibliography 241

Index 245

About the Author 251

Introduction

The story of spirit communication begins many millennia ago at the exact moment when humans started holding funeral rites for their dead. Archaeologists place this date anywhere between 50,000 and 90,000 years ago. We know there was ritual involved in burial; digs have revealed patterns in the way bodies were laid. Many different types of pollens were found around some of the remains, suggesting flowers were present in abundance. Bodies were arranged in exact east/west orientations to correspond with the rise and set of the sun. Others were buried in the fetal position—the same position in which we came into the world.

The question I ask is: Why? Why would these very early humans hold any kind of ritual at all if they didn't believe there was some significance to death? Our ancestors suspected—maybe even assumed—something beyond the physical world, so they took great care to ensure a proper send-off.

Ancestor worship was the earliest form of "religious" or spiritual thought. Humans reached out to the spirits of their ancestors for guidance, for comfort, even for aid in vengeance. The ancient Egyptians were so preoccupied with death, the afterlife, and creating a communicative bond between this world and the next that they spent their entire lives building a society and physical monuments of size and grandeur, all in preparation for the crossover process. World religions evolved with the sole purpose of preparing its members for what comes after death.

For many thousands of years, humans yearned to communicate with the spirit world, but on Friday, March 31, 1848, the spirit world spoke back.

I don't wish to suggest this was the first case of the spirit world speaking to our world. Religious texts and folklore are full of accounts of spirits coming to our physical plane to deliver messages, to offer guidance, to answer questions, or maybe even to scare us (as in the case of hauntings). But March 31, 1848 was different in many ways. This particular form of communication wasn't about touching the hand of one's creator; it was about touching the hand of a regular person who had passed on. This communication started a movement.

On the evening of that fateful day in Hydesville, New York—about 20 miles outside the city of Rochester, in a small farmhouse that had a reputation for being haunted—the Fox family made a connection with the spirit world. John and Margaret Fox and their two daughters, Kate and Margaretta, had only been living in the house for four months when they first heard a strange knocking sound on the walls and disembodied footsteps throughout the home. Some of the raps were subtle; others were strong enough to shake the frames of the beds they slept in. The Fox sisters detected some kind of personality to the knocking and so they gave it a name: Mr. Splitfoot.

According to an account written by Margaret Fox on April 4 of that same year, the Fox family went to bed early that Friday evening—they were determined not to let the knocking disturb their sleep as it had done so often over the previous two weeks. Margaret had already suspected the house was haunted by some restless spirit, but she didn't know what her family could do to get peace in their home. That night, the unusual rapping started again. But this time the Fox sisters played along. A series of knocks sounded from the wall, and the two sisters snapped their fingers in the same pattern. Then came the breakthrough. While lying in her bed, 11-year-old Kate Fox said, "Mr. Splitfoot, do as I do," and she clapped her hands several times. The knocks from the wall repeated the pattern. Then 15-year-old Margaretta joined the game and said, "Now, do just as I do. Count one, two, three, four," she clapped her hands with each number she announced. Again the knocks repeated the pattern. What started as delight in establishing communication quickly turned to horror at the implication of what this all meant. The girls were "talking" to a dead person. They were petrified.

Margaret Fox overheard the exchange and sought her own proof. She asked the presence to sound out the ages of her children. The knocks sounded out each age with a pause in between to differentiate the answers. Mrs. Fox then worked out a system where two knocks meant "yes," and silence meant "no." Through a series of questions, she was able to determine that this was not a living person, but a spirit, and that the spirit had died in an untimely manner in the house. Mrs. Fox called over her nearest neighbor, Mrs. Redfield, to witness the phenomenon. At first she thought this was the children's imagination, but when she arrived, she found the two girls scared, pale, and shaking in their beds. Mrs. Redfield heard the knocks for herself, then she fetched her husband. Soon, other neighbors were summoned, and by Sunday, hundreds had witnessed questions being answered by knocks on the wall. Through this system of knocks, they learned this person was murdered in the house for his money and then buried nearby.

In the case of the Fox sisters, the house was the spirit communication device. The wood in the walls bridged the gap between the physical world and the spirit world to enable communication. This single event and location is credited as being the birth of the modern spiritualist movement—a movement that encourages spirit communication through mediumship.

For the psychically sensitive, this communication may happen naturally, without assistance from any devices. I've spoken with some world-renowned psychic mediums who have told me they can talk with spirits in very much the same manner that they spoke with me. I'm not so lucky. Although these same psychics have told me that we all have the ability, I don't feel I do; or if I do, I don't know how to tap into it.

Many tools have been developed, altered, or acquired for use in spirit communication over the centuries, and some have even gone mainstream, making appearances in movies and novels. Some of these tools are so well known they can be found on toy store or bookstore shelves around the world. Others are more obscure.

To some people, these tools are just games—something to spur a child's fancy. For others, they're oracles to be consulted on issues ranging from the mundane to life and death. Many use these devices for divination—trying to learn what the future may hold. And some make these tools part of their sorcery and magic, using the devices to focus their intent and effect a specific outcome. Then there are those who practice spirit communication—using these devices to try to talk to the dead.

My fascination with this subject began in childhood when I first learned that I had friends who lived in real haunted houses. I never got to see these ghosts, but my friends were sincere in their descriptions. If the ghosts are there, then there must be a way to communicate with them.

I wanted to explore the many methods and techniques that have been used by so many to try to reach across the veil. I wanted to understand the history of these devices, how they came to be used for spirit communication, and what results people were getting. And if there is a scientific explanation, I wanted to understand that perspective as well.

Proof is the point we reach when we have enough evidence to support a claim. The amount and nature of the evidence required to reach proof is different for each of us. Many people ultimately do find their proof from various spirit communication devices. Some people make what they perceive as spirit contact. The messages are meaningful and, in some cases, life-changing.

Through speaking with scientists, clergy, psychologists, psychics, device manufacturers, and many users of these mediumistic tools and techniques, we'll uncover the evidence and try each device. Bring your open mind—you'll find some surprises.

A note on some of the examples and references in this book: As you go through these chapters, you will see there are many audio, video, and image samples discussed. I have set up a special place on the Web to provide direct links to just about every example mentioned in these pages. Go to *www.ghostvillage.com/spiritcommunication* to experience some of the phenomena you're reading about.

"I know that whenever I use a Ouija board or whenever I do a séance, communicating with spirits gives you a sense of your own immortality. You can seek their help, and when you die, someone out there is going to seek yours—so it's a continuous loop of immortality—of becoming God, if you will."

Talking Boards

Saturday, April 10, 2004, in the early afternoon, I pulled out of my driveway and started the hour-long drive north to Salem, Massachusetts. Salem is both famous and infamous among New Age circles. The Witch trials of 1692 certainly gave the town its infamy, but facets of almost every part of New Age culture and subculture dwell somewhere in Salem, making it a destination for occult practitioners and the curious. I was on my way to meet with Bob Murch at his home. Murch is a "talking board" historian, collector, and manufacturer. The talking board—also known as "spirit board" or "Witch board," but best known by its brand name, Ouija board—has become an institution unto itself.

That Saturday was one of those early New England spring days where the weather was warm and the sun shone through a nearly cloudless sky. We get one or two premature shots of these warm days after long, cold winters, and everyone emerges from their hibernations to be outside for as long as possible. The local parks I passed were filled with people and their kids. My windows were down, and my radio was up—it felt good to leave winter behind.

It was also the day before Easter. I haven't considered myself Catholic, much less any religion, in well over a decade, but now

I was embarking on my own spiritual journey. I was going to not only explore the devices people use to communicate with spirits, but to also try these devices myself. I felt some trepidation about jumping into these activities because, though I have studied and written about these subjects before, I have always done so as a sideline observer. I blame it on a little leftover Catholic guilt. But this time, I was rolling up my sleeves and getting involved.

During my drive, I thought about how I used to use a Ouija board when I was about 10 years old and living in Newtown, Connecticut. Two of my friends and I would sleep over at each others' houses and use the board late into the night. We certainly believed we established contact with various spirits back then. Many messages were spelled out, names were given—nothing that I felt was indisputable proof, but certainly enough to raise the hairs on our necks.

I credit the "game" with launching my curiosity into the supernatural. But I also remember some of the warnings priests and nuns would give us in Catholic Christian Doctrine (CCD)—the Catholic version of Sunday School—about communing with the occult and how it leads to dire consequences for our souls, committing them to hell. I didn't buy the notion then; I certainly don't buy it now.

As I drew closer to Salem, I thought about what I wanted to learn about the game, the device, or whatever one prefers to call it. My thoughts were broken by the sound of some motorcycles rumbling up to pass me on the highway. These were among the first motorcycles of the season. I glanced over; they were both Harley-Davidsons. As the riders passed, I saw the backs of their jackets. Either the members or the jackets were new, because the white and red parts of the letters were sharp and bright: Hell's Angels Motorcycle Club.

Driving on Route 114 through downtown Peabody (pronounced *PEE-buddy*, for you out-of-towners) and then into Salem is slow-going during rush hour. Every October, Salem receives an influx of hundreds of thousands of supernatural tourists, making driving there especially unbearable; some have called Salem in October "Mardi Gras for Witches." Fortunately, I didn't have to contend with that. I wound through the streets of downtown Salem until I found the right side street. Murch's house is quaint and set back just far enough from the small alley to offer some privacy. He greeted me at the door with a smile and a handshake. Murch is a 30-year-old professional who lights up with energy when talking about Ouija. He keeps his head nearly shaved, and his dress is typical casual New Englander: jeans and a light sweater. The only sign that he might be into anything even remotely offbeat is the dark earrings he has hanging from each lobe.

Bob Murch with some of the many spirit boards in his collection. Photo by Marc Vasconcellos.

Inside, his home is decorated with framed Ouija artifacts, such as a *Saturday Evening Post* magazine cover from May 1, 1920, featuring a Norman Rockwell painting of a young couple with their hands resting on the message indicator, or *planchette*, of the Ouija board. The man and woman are seated in facing chairs with their knees touching, and the woman is looking off into nowhere, seemingly in awe of the mysticism at work, while the man is looking intently at the woman. Two autographs adorn the framed cover; under the woman, Kathy Fuld signed her name, and under the man, Stuart Fuld left his mark. I would soon learn the significance of these autographs being together. Other frames in Murch's home contain old advertisements for the board game, box covers from one of the early Ouija boards, and other artifacts from the 20th century featuring Ouija.

"You have to remember the Ouija board wasn't seen as occult back in the first half of the 20th century," Murch said. "But it broke a lot of rules, and not in the way that you think. It broke rules in a sense that men and women were not supposed to be sitting that close on a date, but you had to, to play this game. Your knees were touching, your hands were touching, you got to put down the lights. There's a lot behind that. There was no Twister back then."

"This is really your passion," I said.

"Definitely."

The talking board story starts with an old Witchcraft conjuring method that involved writing the alphabet and numbers on pieces of paper, then resting the fingers on an upside-down glass or cup that would drift toward the letters and numbers to spell out messages. It's difficult to put an exact date on this method, because it was passed along as an oral tradition in many cases, but the Witches I spoke with believe it predates commercial talking boards by at least a few centuries. This early method led to the first talking boards, which had their first mention in print in the *New York Tribune* on March 28, 1886. The article described a rectangular board with letters and numbers on it, which was used to spell out messages. The article never said the communications were coming from the spirit world, but it did imply that some felt it was a "witching" thing.

The Ouija board story starts on May 28, 1890, when the Kennard Novelty Company filed for patent No. 446,054 on the Ouija "Egyptian Luck Board."

The Kennard Novelty Company of Baltimore, Maryland, consisted of Charles Kennard, Harry Welles Rusk, Colonel Washington Bowie, Elijah J. Bond, and William Fuld. All of these men were Masons, and it's assumed their coming together occurred within the secretive society. Some also believe the design of the Ouija board incorporates some Masonic elements, such as its sun and moon and the arc of the letters on the board.

Kennard offered the new company leftover land and buildings from a failed fertilizer business venture—his donation of real estate was enough to get his name on the company letterhead and get him the title of president. Rusk, a prominent patent attorney and politician, used his political influence and legal savvy to expedite patent filing and approval. Col. Bowie brought the money to invest in the products and marketing. Elijah Bond, another patent attorney, offered more legal expertise, and Fuld brought his sharp, young, game-inventor's mind and played a big role in production. Their initial operations were housed at 220 South Charles Street in Baltimore.

The Kennard Novelty Company sold its first Ouija board in 1891. The game looked very similar to today's modern version, except that it was printed on real wood. The planchette was also made of real wood and was only a pointer—there was no hole in the middle. The game was starting to move off the shelves, but business operations wouldn't stay at Kennard's helm for very long. By the end of 1891, Charles Kennard was removed as president—he was a subpar businessman. The company moved operations to 909 East Pratt Street, and the name changed to The Ouija Novelty Company, with Col. Bowie and William Fuld in charge. Fuld was only 21 years old at the time.

Fuld is often credited with the invention of the Ouija board. But even though it was Fuld who seized the opportunity, the "inventor" distinction may be too generous. However, he's certainly the father of the board, as his vision and savvy promoted the game into millions of homes around the world.

"Lots of people were involved with the invention of the Ouija board," Murch said. He showed me around his downstairs office—framed pictures of different members of Fuld's family adorned the walls, including one photograph of William Fuld sitting behind the Ouija board. The picture showed a man in his 30s with a mustache, glasses, and sharp eyes under those glasses. His short, jet-black hair was parted in the middle and held down with some brand of pomade. He was thin and seemed to carry himself with an air of intelligence.

Murch talked about how the dejected Kennard started his own talking board company after being removed from the Kennard Novelty Company. Kennard's board was called the *Volo*, but he never filed for a trademark. Bowie and Fuld placed an exact copy of Kennard's Volo on the back side of their Ouija board; consumers could get two boards for the price of one, and Kennard was driven out of business.

One of the Kennard Novelty Company's earliest Ouija boards (circa 1895) from Bob Murch's collection. Photo by Jeff Belanger.

William Fuld's brother Isaac also entered the business, but in 1901, disputes over the operations erupted, the courts were involved, and a Fuld family rift was set firmly in place. Isaac Fuld left the company and dropped all contact with his brother's side of the family. Isaac Fuld started the *Oriole* board, an almost exact replica of the Ouija board, though consumer support of the Oriole was nowhere near what it was for Ouija.

When Murch started his research, he contacted Kathy Fuld, granddaughter of William, to see what the family could offer to a very muddied history of such a popular game. Likewise, he got in touch with Stuart Fuld, grandson of Isaac. He would eventually arrange a meeting between both cousins in Baltimore,

Isaac Fuld's short-lived Oriole board. Photo by Jeff Belanger.

in 1997—a meeting that would mark the end of a 96-year family feud. At this meeting, Kathy and Stuart signed the cover of Murch's *Saturday Evening Post.*

So from the Fuld family's perspective, does it work? Murch said, "When people used to ask the Fulds if the Ouija board really worked, they would look around at their mansion and say, 'It worked for us!'" The more Murch and I spoke about Fuld and the Ouija, the more it became clear that Fuld was a marketing genius.

Murch showed me his collection of talking boards. I had no idea they were collector's items. I also had no idea how many different talking boards were manufactured to compete with the Ouija board. Some of the other boards bore names such as: Oriole, Magic Marvel, Rajah, Swami, Hasko Mystic Board, The Wireless Messenger, Yogee, Mystic Genii Board, and many others. He said many were worth $200–$300, depending on the board and its condition; however, a few boards were worth $1,000-plus, such as the Electric Mystifying Oracle—Fuld's masterpiece, though it didn't sell that well. The planchette, powered by a dry cell battery, lit up when it passed over contact points near each letter. The board came out in 1930, and its $3.50-plus price tag was a bit too high for Depression-era customers. This may explain why few were produced and why even fewer survive today.

The Ouija brand was a hot commodity, and Fuld pushed it as far as he could. His company even marketed a product called "Ouija Oil," a rub-on ointment to treat rheumatoid arthritis. Murch showed me black-and-white photos of the Ouija board as it appeared in an episode of the television show *Dennis the Menace* (1959–1963) and in the 1960 movie *13 Ghosts*. Ouija's popularity hit an all-time peak in 1967, when it became the first board game to outsell *Monopoly*.

The Ouija board has been a part of our culture and subculture for the last century. Murch said, "With a Ouija board, the story is so simple from now looking back. But you get a totally different story if you start backwards and try to work your way to today. The Ouija board has its own life, it's got its own pop culture that's evolved all around it, regardless of its own history. So there are these parallel stories running at the same time, and they cross, but you have to be careful because what most people think is fact are just these parallel stories"—parallel stories about its origin, about what it can and can't do, and about what has happened to people who use them.

"Ouijastitions" is a term Murch uses to describe some of the lore around spirit boards. For example, regarding the very name "Ouija," some claim it comes from the French word for "yes," *oui*, and the German word for "yes," *ja*. Another story suggests "Ouija" is the Egyptian word for "luck." It isn't. Then there is the fabled Moroccan city of Oujda—the board may have been named after that. Other lore says Charles Kennard sat down and used the board with his girlfriend and asked the board to name itself, and O-U-I-J-A is what was spelled out.

"We just don't know," Murch said.

Considering the widespread sales success of the game, it's possible the origins of the name may have been too boring for something so mysterious, so Fuld never denied nor confirmed any story any person wanted to make up about the history of the board.

"The more mystery the better," I said.

"Exactly," Murch replied.

In 1973, Ouija lore turned dark. Writer William Peter Blatty penned *The Exorcist*, a movie that still scares the hell out of people today. This was the first implication that an evil spirit (such as the one Blatty eloquently monikered "Captain Howdy") could use the Ouija board as a doorway to possess a victim. The movie has made many equate talking boards with demonic possession ever since.

The Exorcist was loosely based on some real events involving a 13-year-old boy from Cottage City, Maryland, whom the newspapers and the priests involved in the eventual exorcisms publicly referred to as "Roland Doe" (son of Mr. and Mrs. John Doe) from nearby Mount Rainier, Maryland. According to the journal of one of these priests, in January of 1949, Roland and his "Aunt Tillie" used a Ouija board together on several occasions. Aunt Tillie had an interest in the Spiritualist movement and showed Roland how to use the board. On January 26, 1949, Aunt Tillie died of multiple sclerosis, and that's when the allegedly demonic trouble began. Roland was treated in both Maryland and St. Louis by both doctors and clergy. It was later discovered that Roland had a history of psychological problems. Though the many priests and Protestant clergy who were involved with the exorcisms may have mentioned the Ouija board, they never named the device as the trigger that started the demonic trouble. It was Blatty who focused in on the board, because that made for a better story.

As years passed after *The Exorcist*, the American psyche calmed and associated Ouija less with demonic possession. Sales efforts continued for Parker Brothers, which was then manufacturing the game in Salem, Massachusetts. Production in Salem continued until Hasbro bought Parker Brothers in 1991.

Bob Murch then explained how he continued the mysterious marketing tradition with *his* version of the spirit board called *Cryptique*, which first hit the shelves in 1999. "When we first marketed Cryptique, it was a Cryptique *talking* board. No one cared; it was horrible. As soon as we changed it to the Cryptique *spirit* board from Salem, Massachusetts, we got a huge response; that's what got us really big—'spirit board.'"

When compared to Hasbro's latest incarnation of the Ouija board, Cryptique takes a much more occult-friendly approach. The box cover features the winged skull, or colonial death head, on the cover—a symbol taken from old New England gravestones. The letters are scattered around the board, which features the image of a piece of wood taken from Old Burial Hill in Marblehead,

Massachusetts. Even their registered trademark slogan, "Let the Spirit Move You," implies the spirit communication connection.

The Cryptique spirit board. Photo courtesy of Bob Murch.

Sales have increased each year of operation for Murch's company—today they sell thousands per year in various retail outlets, though not all retail outlets are friendly toward talking boards. Wal-Mart won't carry Cryptique, or Hasbro's Ouija. Murch glows when talking about these products. "It's a lot of people's first contact with what they believe to be supernatural and spirits," he said.

Back upstairs, Christian Day joined us, dressed completely in black. Day, 34, is a local Salem Witch, Tarot reader, and graphic designer by trade, who helped Murch with the design of the Cryptique packaging as well as copywriting.

Day appeared on the Showtime series *Bullshit*, featuring Penn and Teller, with Murch and two other Witches from Salem. *Bullshit* was doing an episode on talking boards and used Cryptique as their case study.

"We didn't know the show was called *Bullshit* when they contacted us," Murch said.

"You're kidding," I said.

"No. It was their production company that filmed everything. We didn't know Penn and Teller were involved or anything."

"When did you find out?"

"About two weeks before the show aired, a friend saw a commercial for the show. He called us and said, 'Hey, I see you guys are going to be on this show, *Bullshit*.' I was fuming."

Murch feared the worst for his friendships and for his business. "But in the end, [the show] was pretty easy on us, and our sales went through the roof."

Murch's suspicions were first raised during the filming when the producers asked to blindfold the spirit board users to see if it would still work. Murch said, "We objected because it defeats the purpose of using a spirit board. Obviously at that point, we realized they wanted to disprove it, which doesn't help my business or my passion. I don't want people to stop using them, I think they're great fun, regardless of why they work. But I think half the fun is thinking about why they work."

The producers went through with their blindfold experiment, using two random people in California to film it. The board was turned upside down when the users were blindfolded, and there were no intelligible results. One explanation is that the spirits channel through the board users and, thus, need the users' senses of touch and sight. The other explanation would lean toward the title of Penn and Teller's program. In the end, the show gave Cryptique a big boost in sales, and Murch laughs about it now.

Murch is also a savvy marketer, surely borrowing from William Fuld's playbook. He understands that to some this is just a game, but that many believe this is a tool to contact the dead. He's happy to let his product be whatever it is his customers want it to be. This trick is something talking board makers have been successful at doing for more than a century.

Christian Day is a believer but has a healthy dose of skepticism. I asked him if these things really work to communicate with the dead.

"I don't think the talent is in the Ouija board; I think the talent is in the user," Day said. "I think that you will get out of any psychic experiment what you put into that psychic experiment, and that includes your state of mind. I think it's your open mindedness, your willingness to allow what might happen to happen. I don't think it requires a belief, because spirits, if they exist, exist outside of our belief. It's about just letting yourself relax and not have any preconceived expectations."

In my own preparations for having a séance with a spirit board, I wanted to ask more people more questions.

I called a childhood friend of mine, Rev. Dean Osuch, Minister of Evangelism and Pastor of Mount Pisgah United Methodist Church in Alpharetta, Georgia. I wanted a Christian perspective on talking boards.

Dean and I haven't actually seen each other for more than 10 years, but we do speak frequently on the phone about different religious topics. He's an energetic guy who is passionate about what he does. He's also quick to laugh—a charm that puts people he speaks with at ease. I like discussing occult topics with him because he's never offended by the questions. I didn't think it was fair to come out and ask Dean if these devices are evil, so I posed the question to him this way: "If someone from your church came to you and said his son or daughter was playing with a spirit board, is it okay?"

"What I would do is I would turn to the Scripture and have them look at it," he said. "Instead of giving them the answer, I'd have them discover it on their own and they can come up with their own conclusions. I would turn them to Deuteronomy 18:9–12. Do you want me to read it to you?"

"Yes, I don't have the Bible quite memorized yet."

He laughed. Dean read to me from his New American Standard version of the Old Testament. He prefaced the verses by telling me that in the chapter, Moses is talking to the children of Israel who have just entered the Promised Land. Dean read, "When you come into the land which the Lord your God has given you, you shall not learn to follow the abominations of those nations. There shall not be found among you anyone who makes his son or her daughter pass through the fire or one who practices witchcraft, or a soothsayer, or one who interprets omens, or a sorcerer or one who conjures spells or a medium, or a spiritualist or one who calls up the dead. For all who do these things are an abomination to the Lord."

Dean said, "The term *Ouija board* isn't in the Bible. So what you have to do at this point is look at the Bible and look at the principle of what is being said and apply it to today."

"I guess it doesn't take a Bible scholar to interpret the passage you read and see this game is probably covered there," I said.

Dean laughed again. "Nope, it's pretty spelled out."

Dean never used a Ouija board but admits there was one in his house growing up. He said his concern is when people go to devices or people rather than directly to God for spiritual answers.

Fair enough. Considering Dean was reading from the Old Testament, it's fair to assume there would be many other clergy, both Christian and Jewish, who would agree with Dean's interpretation. Granted, mysticism is an ancient part of even mainstream religions, and I know there are some clergy who believe divination not to be a practice against Scripture, but I also believe those clergy would be in the minority today.

So what about psychologically speaking? The reality is that the pointer does move. I've seen it happen. I've had it happen to me. There are only a few possible explanations as to why the pointer is moving: (1) I'm moving it, (2) you're moving it, (3) we're both collectively moving it, or (4) something otherworldly is moving it.

For possibilities one through three, I contacted Mike Cocchiola, a board-certified behavior analyst based in Woodbury, Connecticut. He's a soft-spoken man who treats people from very young to very old. Cocchiola has never used a talking board but is well aware of what they are.

He drew a comparison between the talking board and something he has seen used and studied in psychology called a "Qwerty board" (QWERTY being the first six letters across a standard typing keyboard). "The Qwerty board was originally meant for people who had difficulty speaking, but at the same time, they were cognizant enough in order to be able to spell something out," Cocchiola said. "Then it broadbanded generally across all people and all settings, so that severely and profoundly retarded people could begin to use them and to speak"—and one of the major issues with using the device arose. He explained, "The Qwerty board was tested out over the course of time, and it was shown that, in actuality, the person facilitating didn't really mean to but was kind of assisting in the process."

Cocchiola described a scenario where one of the board's users was presented with something he might want, such as a drink. To get the drink, he needed to ask for it. He said, "Let's say the person was saying he wanted milk—M-I-L-K, and the person who was assisting them, the facilitator, would actually kind of direct that answer, maybe even subconsciously."

"How does the facilitator help the person using the Qwerty board?" I asked.

"If the person wants milk, the facilitator would actually lift the arm of that person up and allow him to press the M key."

That certainly didn't sound very scientific. Cocchiola explained how the mentally disabled users of the Qwerty board had varying results, depending on who was helping them use the device.

Cocchiola said, "My question is: Scientifically, is there any validity to the Ouija board? Can it be validated that something directs the outcome, other than the two people who have kind of a desired outcome or a desired answer—can that be validated?"

"No, it can't be validated," I said. "However, it can't be invalidated either." All part of the talking board's charm and mystery.

Cocchiola also accepts that these devices do work on a spiritual level for some people. He said, "If you find that the concept works for you, that's okay. Do I have any faith in it for you? Sure. For me, show me the data."

There is no shortage of people with a supernatural talking board experience. For many, it's the first tangible introduction into the occult, spiritualism, and spirit communication. I use the word *tangible* because, for many, the first sense of spirituality comes from early childhood memories of parents teaching us to pray or of going to church. I was taught we go to church to talk to God. But the Ouija board actually talks back. This is eye-opening for many. It certainly was for me.

In collecting talking board encounters, I started with my friends. I asked the question: Did you ever use a Ouija board? A good friend of mine named Roberto Aberasturia had a convincing experience in the fall of 1993, when he was a student at Sacred Heart University in Fairfield, Connecticut. Seeing as how Halloween was only a few weeks away, Roberto and eight of his friends piled into a dorm room with a Ouija board to help get into the spirit (pun intended) of the season. Two girls used the board while Roberto and five others watched from various places around the room.

"Did you try using the board, too?" I asked.

"No," he said. "I heard that the spirits use the person as the channel, and I didn't want that. I don't like anybody controlling my body."

After people in the group asked a series of basic questions like, "Are there any spirits present?" "Where is my grandmother?" and "How old is she?" Roberto thought the answers ambiguous.

"I wanted proof that this was real," he said. "I purposely sat at the end or the last seat facing my two friends who were working the Ouija board, but I made sure that nobody was behind me because my whole aim going into this thing was to see if it was actually accurate, if it was for real. I took my watch off and I put it right behind the seat of one of my college roommates. I'm 100 percent positive that nobody saw where I put the watch, and the two girls that were using the Ouija board had their eyes fixated on the board, so there was no way they saw me place the watch there. And then I asked the board if it could tell me where my watch was."

"So you tested it." I said.

"Exactly," he said. "At that point the Ouija board began to spell out T-E-S-T, so I presumed it was asking me *Is this a test?* I said, 'Yes, it is a test.' And then it spelled out C-H-A-I-R. And I said, 'Okay, chair,' that's kind of a vague response. I asked it, 'Okay, whose chair is it on?' It spelled S-C-O-T-T, and that was the guy's chair that I put my watch behind, and that's who was sitting on the chair at the time. At that point I just picked up my watch, put it on, and walked out of the room, because I knew this thing wasn't a hoax—there was something real behind it. Again, nobody saw me, and I didn't give the answer."

For Roberto, the *Ouija* board gave him the proof he asked for. Once proof is established for someone, messages that come from the device definitely carry more weight.

Such is the case with Maggie Judd from Ontario, who e-mailed me at Ghostvillage.com regarding what she believes was a premonition she received from her Ouija board. She said, "Years ago, a friend and I were goofing around with a Ouija board. Being a bit ignorant of these things, I asked it how old I would be when I died and how it would happen. [The board] replied that I would be 16 and that I would die in a car accident. A month or two after I turned 16, my parents asked me if I wanted to go out with them the next day to run errands. I said yes. That next morning, I woke up to discover that my parents left without me—I was annoyed. An hour after I woke up, my mother called me from the hospital. They had been hit by a transport truck an hour earlier. When I asked why they had left without me, my mom replied that she and my dad had tried for half an hour to get me up and then gave up. What makes it so scary is where the truck had hit. My one brother had to sit behind my mom, so had I been in that car, I would have been sitting behind my dad. The transport truck hit the car on the driver's side, almost imploding on the driver's and left backseat side—where I would have been."

Talking boards offer psychic evidence, premonitions, and sometimes even poetry. There was a band in Salem, Massachusetts, called Coven 13 who released an album titled *Book of Shadows* in 1998, featuring the song "Ophelia's Lament." While working on that piece, the band had already laid down the music, but they were stuck trying to come up with lyrics for the bridge of the song. They used a Ouija board in the studio to write the lyrics.

Shawn Poirier, High Priest of The Salem Witches, was in the studio during the recording.

"What happened when you took out the Ouija board?" I asked.

"We were in contact with Ophelia—either the actual person that may have lived or the thought form or the energy of Ophelia," Poirier said. "When we wrote down the message, we gave it to Teisan [one of the band's founders] and he said, 'Okay, let's give it a try,' and it matched every beat—it matched perfectly within the measure of the music. So the spirits know. We really made genuine contact."

Poirier is a psychic intuitive who witnessed more than just music being made that day. He said, "While they were composing the song, I had no idea they were in the other room working on the music. And at the time, a Christmas tree was up. The Christmas tree turned into a glass column, and I saw this beautiful woman in white just spiraling in the tree. I said, 'What are you guys doing in there?' They said, 'We're working on a song dedicated to Ophelia,' so we believe that she is with us in that song."

After speaking with all of these individuals, it was my turn to try the spirit board.

"I don't want you using these things in the house," my wife, Megan, said.

"Why not?"

"Not that I'm superstitious, but if something comes through, I don't want it in our house," she said.

Okay, fair enough. For my first experiment, I would use the board alone outside. I chose the Cryptique board and went in my backyard to sit on a stone wall in the woods behind my house. It was early afternoon on a Tuesday—our first clear day after several days of rain. I sat down in the warm sun and smelled the scent of the freshly watered woods. I rested my hands on the tombstone-shaped pointer of the Cryptique board.

"Are there any spirits present?" I asked.

At the very instant I finished asking the question, a loud *whoosh* of wind blew through the area where I was sitting. A blast of wind in the woods behind my house is by no means an anomaly, but I thought the blast was well-timed. I waited about two minutes and asked again, but the message indicator never moved.

I admit I felt a little self-conscious. What if a neighbor saw me sitting in the woods with a spirit board? They would think I'm even stranger than they already do. I looked around a few times and was satisfied I wasn't being watched. I didn't feel scared; I didn't really feel anything.

"Are there any spirits present?" I asked again. I waited about five minutes, but nothing happened with the board.

My next move was to try again with a partner. For my spirit board guide, I chose Shawn Poirier. Back to Salem I went. The date was Tuesday, May 12, 2004.

Poirier makes his living giving psychic readings and teaching Witchcraft. I arrived at his home in the afternoon and was greeted by Shawn, dressed completely in black. He's in his mid-30s, has long dark hair, a goatee, and dark eye shadow over each eye. His Massachusetts accent gave away that he was raised locally. His home was adorned with death masks; Witch symbols, such as pentagrams; mannequins dressed as Witches; and a collection of various dolls behind a glass case.

I sat down at his kitchen table and a black cat name Ka rubbed against my leg. I thought the black cat was a nice touch. A 1966 version of the Parker Brothers Ouija board was waiting for us on the table.

"Why is it important for people to communicate with spirits?" I asked.

"I think it's important because it lets you know that you're going to go on," Poirier said. "I know that whenever I use a Ouija board or whenever I do a séance, communicating with spirits gives you a sense of your own immortality. You can seek their help, and when you die, someone out there is going to seek yours—so it's a continuous loop of immortality—of becoming God, if you will."

Poirier gave me the metaphysical perspective on talking boards. He was raised in a family of Witches; both his grandmothers practiced Witchcraft, as did his parents. So from a young age, he studied spells and spirit communication. He was around 10 years of age when he first started using the Ouija board as a tool for communication. Eventually, Poirier discovered he could receive messages directly from spirits by simply concentrating on the Ouija board at his hands. He used the board to focus, but he didn't need the pointer to get messages. In a sense, the board was like training wheels that helped Poirier develop his psychic communication skills.

"Who can we contact with a talking board?" I asked.

"You can talk to not only humans, you can talk to other creatures on the board," he said. "Other elemental creatures or creatures that are not quite human or creatures that are alien. And people think that they're dark, but they're not. They just have a different sense of morality."

For many occult practitioners, this lower elemental attraction is the primary concern with using talking boards. Many warned me to be careful about heeding advice when communicating with these lower creatures.

"You can also contact the living with the board," Shawn said.

"The living? How?"

"If I wanted to contact you," Poirier said. "I could pull you into the screen of my mind—if we had a close connection—and I could say 'Jeff...call me. Let me know you're okay.' If I wasn't psychic, the board would start spelling what you're doing. What I would do is just kind of pull you in, jump into you, and look at life through your eyes to make sure you didn't need help. So you can actually conjure living people with the Ouija board too. All you have to do is put their picture and a piece of their hair on the board, or a piece of their clothing or handwriting."

He also said the board can be used for spellcasting in Witchcraft. Poirier's impression of the board is that it's a focusing tool for psychic energy. The user's intent is what makes this a tool for spirit communication, conjuring, or spellcasting.

"Can spirit boards be dangerous?" I asked.

"They are definitely doors to unlock things," Poirier said. "Not so much in the spirit world, but in the mind. If a person is in a state of mourning or grieving or they can't deal with the death of someone, and they approach a vehicle or a medium that's designed specifically for the purpose of tapping those thoughts and those emotions, of course they're going to panic. The emotions are too hot. But the board itself cannot harm anyone. If you have Gandhi on a board, you're going to get good spirits. If you get Adolf Hitler on the board, of course you're going to get lesser or bad spirits. There's a saying in magic that like draws to like. It's one of the oldest forms of magic—sympathetic magic. And the spirits that are drawn to you are the spirits that are most like you."

We were ready to give the board a try. The base of Poirier's board was made of composite wood and the planchette had a metal nail in the middle of the plastic window to point to an exact spot below.

"You want to get one white candle and one black candle," Poirier said. "White scientifically puts out energy, so you're sending out good thoughts to surround yourself in a protective circle. The black scientifically draws in light or information. So you're polarizing the board.

"On the back of the board, you might want to draw some kind of symbol with your finger, like a pentacle, or cross if you're Christian, or a Star of David, or the name of a person that you just want to talk to."

Poirier traced both a pentacle and a cross. I'm not sure if he was just demonstrating or felt strongly about both symbols.

We each rubbed our hands together quickly to get the energy flowing, then shook them out as if we just washed our hands but there were no towels to dry them on. Finally, we took three deep breaths, then each placed one hand on the planchette. Shawn directed me to ask the questions and drive the experience. He closed his eyes. I had no expectations for this session. I wanted proof, but I would settle for evidence.

"Are there any spirits present who want to communicate with us?" I asked. Now I felt a little tingle on the back of my neck, as though someone was standing behind me. My breathing increased—something I didn't notice until Shawn pointed it out. I was concentrating on my fingers being energized.

We waited. Maybe 30 seconds went by and the planchette started to move. Slow and steady the pointer made a loop around the inside of the board then went down and stopped at the number 3 at the bottom.

"Are there three spirits present?" I asked.

The planchette moved almost instantly to "Yes." I asked for the names of the spirits to be spelled out, but the planchette didn't move.

"Are there any messages for us?" I asked.

The pointer moved down to the letter P then up to the letter C. It stopped on C.

"Has anyone in your family passed who could be associated with the letter C?" Shawn asked.

I thought about it. My grandfather on my mother's side was named Joseph, but his friends all knew him as Chet. I knew him simply as "Paw." The only other "C" in my family was my great uncle Charlie—my grandfather's brother. I didn't give any names to Poirier; I waited for the board to tell me more.

"Can you give us more information?" I asked of the board.

The planchette moved directly in between "Yes" and "No"— directly over the "Ouija" logo. And there it stayed. Shawn used his intuitive abilities after a few minutes of no movement.

"I'm sensing a lot of male energy around you," Poirier said. "And I'm getting the name Charlie. Charlie is a stubborn spirit."

The planchette felt as if it was attached to the board, like it was very heavy. I gently tried to nudge it, but nothing moved. The minutes were going by and the planchette stayed this way.

"Are there any messages for us?" I asked again. A split second after I asked, some dogs outside barked ferociously for only a moment.

We sat for five more minutes with our hands resting on the planchette, but it wouldn't budge.

"How do we end this session?" I asked.

Poirier flipped over the planchette, then threw some salt from a nearby jar onto the board. "The energies are broken up by the salt."

We talked about the movement of the pointer across the board. I can tell you in all honesty I didn't push the planchette. And if Poirier was pushing it, I would imagine he would have been a lot more sensational and creative than just the letters P and C. When the planchette did move, I could almost sense its movement before it happened. My fingers were just resting on the pointer—certainly not enough to affect its direction. We even did an experiment where we both tried to move the pointer around. I could tell we were fighting each other—the movement wasn't smooth like it was during the session.

We took a break and were ready to try again.

Shawn walked over to a corner of the kitchen and picked up a human skull. "Robert, this is Jeff. He's friendly," Poirier said.

Yes, it was a real human skull—having visited the Catacomb Museum in Paris and seeing hundreds of thousands of human skulls first-hand, I know this was real. It didn't look like a medical skull either—it was not bleached white like the one in high-school biology class. The top of the skull had been sawed off with a precision instrument and was resting on the bottom portion. The skull didn't have its lower mandible either. Poirier set the skull down so the upper portion of the jaw was just above the "Ouija" logo.

We were going to try communication again—but this time Poirier wanted to communicate directly with the spirit of Robert.

"Robert, I want you to move the planchette around so Jeff can get a feel for the board," Poirier said.

We set our hands on the planchette as we did before, and the movement started almost immediately. It stopped on C again. Poirier and I both laughed, but then it went back to moving around the board in an up-and-down pattern. A few times the planchette came up and touched the skull before going back to its now-familiar pattern. This went on for about two to three minutes before we stopped.

Poirier flipped both the Ouija board and the planchette over on their tops to break the connection. I thanked him for meeting with me and thought about what I had witnessed, during my drive home.

The planchette had moved—I believe that—and it held fast for more than five minutes. During our two sessions, I tried to keep my mind clear and my attention focused. I can never say with certainty that Poirier wasn't pushing the planchette (just as he can't say I wasn't pushing it), but because the session wasn't over-the-top, I just don't believe my guide was out to dupe me.

I believe we made some kind of spirit connection. I don't have firsthand proof, but I have my hunch. The first time I used a talking board as a child, I thought it was a game—granted, a game that sparked a lot of curiosity. Now I know it's so much more. It's a piece of Americana, it's a psychic focusing tool, it's a communication device, and above all, it's an enigma.

" The Magician card is reaching up into the world of Heaven and pointing to the world of Earth. It's a very specific answer to your question, because the Magician is **a physical channel** for spirits to come into the physical world. "

Tarot Cards

I don't consider myself an art snob by any stretch of the imagination, but I certainly appreciate visiting museums. I love walking the great halls and looking at the paintings—especially when it's quiet and not too crowded and you can hear your footsteps echo around the high ceilings. I remember walking through the Boston Museum of Fine Art one summer day in 2003 and seeing one specific painting, by itself, on a stark wall. The canvas was mostly white with a fat streak of red paint going across it—and that was the painting. Nothing more. I stared. I cocked my head like a golden retriever looking at his master naked. *Huh? That's not art, is it? I mean I could do that right now with no practice and no talent. Just gimme a brush and some red paint.* This work meant nothing to me. Then an elderly woman, dressed impeccably and smelling of old money, walked up next to me to admire the same painting. She drew in a breath, held her hand to her mouth, and whispered "Oh my" into her palm. I shrugged and moved on.

A week before writing this, I was in London for a few days and stopped in the National Gallery at Trafalgar Square. I immediately went to the Rembrandt room. I was completely taken by his *Self Portrait at the Age of 63* (painted in 1669). His wizened and weathered face was contrasted by such soulful eyes—eyes that have guided his hand to create some incredible master-pieces throughout his life. In the painting, he's dressed simply, a brown hat set back on his receding hairline with tufts of gray hair spilling out from under it, and his hands are resting on his slightly portly belly. There's no pretension at all in Rembrandt's image of himself. I stared in quiet awe until someone walked by in front of me, breaking my gaze. She walked right past this painting and out into another room of the museum. *How can you miss this?* I thought.

Like art, spirit communication is all about messages, feel-ings, and many times images—channeling them, receiving them, and interpreting the meaning. Tarot cards are all about complex messages and all about the artwork. Modern tarot users first need to find a deck with pictures that speak to them personally, and then they can truly work with the cards and explore what messages lie in the shuffles, flips, and spreads.

Does tarot's message/magic come from within? From ran-dom chance? Or is it directed by spirits? The answers to these questions are different for each person who consults a tarot deck—but they are questions that must be answered on the indi-vidual level in order to work with these cards.

Tarot cards were first manufactured sometime between 1440 and 1445 C.E. in Northern Italy, purely as a card game for noblemen. Certainly before 1440 there were cards that were coming together to look like predecessors to tarot decks, such as a 56-card deck produced in 1423 that featured court cards and was being printed by woodblocks that were then colored in with stencils. This new process drastically reduced the time it took to create a deck, and thus also reduced the cost, compared with older decks, where each card of each deck had to be hand-painted. This made playing cards more accessible to the masses, who not only used the cards for recreational games but also for gambling, much to the chagrin of the church.

In 1442, in an accounting book belonging to the prominent D'Este family in the court of the Marquis of Mantua, there is a reference to an artist being commissioned for the development of four decks of *trionfi*. This is the first documentation of "tarot," and these decks contained the suits of Cups, Swords, Coins, and Batons.

Originally called *carte da trionfi* (cards of the triumphs), the decks were elaborately painted with medieval and Renaissance artwork, and the game played with them was similar to our modern game of bridge. What we know today as the *Major Arcana*, the set of cards not assigned to any of the four suits, were the trump cards. By 1445, the game was becoming very popular among the Milanese and other northern Italian aristocrats; from there, the game and cards would eventually filter down to the masses.

Early in the 1500s, in Northern Italy, the name of the cards evolved to *tarocchi*, which is the plural of *tarocco*—a term whose meaning has eluded historians. Some believe its roots are ancient Italian. Others believe the word is from the Arabic *taraqa*, meaning "to hammer." The credit for "tarot" may go to French author Francois Rabelais who, in 1534, wrote *The Five Books of Gargantua and Pantagruel*. In his work, there was a character named Gargantua who played a game called *tarau*. The French evolved the word to *tarot*.

Prior to 1781, there are some vague references to tarot being used for fortune telling/cartomancy, but in 1781, we find the first documentations of tarot being used for divination in Antoine Court de Gébelin's essay titled "Concerning the Game of Tarots" and Louis-Raphaël-Lucrèce De Mellet's essay "Studies in Tarots." These two documents would make much of the world forever equate tarot with the occult.

Court de Gébelin's essay discusses an event that took place in the mid-1770s when he was watching a friend playing the game of tarot and was struck with a sense of knowing the allegorical origins of the cards. His epiphany led him to draw conclusions such as the Chariot card depicted the Egyptian god Osiris, the Devil represented the Egyptian god Set, and Judgment showed the creation of the world. In every other trump card, he also drew a reference to ancient Egypt. He also believed the four suits represented groups or classes of people. His arguments were quickly dismissed as pure conjecture.

In "Studies in Tarots," De Mellet also claimed tarot's origins were ancient Egyptian, but his arguments were more esoteric. By emulating Egyptian priests, he created a method of reading tarot in a 10-card spread. He developed meanings for the four suits, such as Swords foretold of poverty, worry, death, and pain; Wands represented success, fortune, and money; Cups told of happiness and contentment; and Pentacles meant luck. De Mellet's essay was highly sought-after and helped launch the public's interest in using tarot as much more than just a card game.

Today there are thousands of decks in circulation with more being produced all the time. Tarot publishing has exploded in the last 15 to 20 years. Before the 1980s, there were really only a few decks that were widely available. Aleister Crowley's Thoth Tarot is certainly one well-known deck; but by far the most instantly recognizable and the all-time best-selling deck is the Rider-Waite Tarot—though it probably would have been more fair to call it the "Rider-Waite-Smith" deck. Named for Rider & Company of London, the company who published the deck in 1910, it was developed by occult scholar and member of The Order of the Golden Dawn, Dr. Arthur Edward Waite, and designed under Waite's direction by artist Pamela Colman Smith, who was also a member of the Golden Dawn. The Order of the Golden Dawn was founded in 1887 as a training ground into esoteric traditions such as Kabbalah, alchemy, and other Western mysteries. Tarot was a natural way for Waite and others to explore and teach these mysteries through a series of images. This deck was the first tarot deck to assign emblematic designs to all of the cards in the deck, not just the Major Arcana and the face cards of each suit. Rider-Waite was also the first tarot deck I ever bought, because the colorful image of the Fool on the box, dressed in medieval attire and looking skyward as he is about to step off a cliff in the mountains, was immediately recognizable to me.

Tarot decks are typically comprised of 78 cards divided into the Greater or Major Arcana and the Lesser or Minor Arcana (*arcana* meaning a deep secret, or mystery). The Major Arcana consists of 22 numbered face cards (0 through 21). In my Rider-Waite deck, the Major Arcana includes: the Magician, the High Priestess, the Empress, the Emperor, the Heirophant, the Lovers, the Chariot, Strength, the Hermit, Wheel of Fortune, Justice, the Hanged Man, Death, Temperance, the Devil, the Tower, the Star, the Moon, the Sun, the Last Judgment, the World, and the Fool. The Lesser Arcana includes the four suits of the Tarot. The traditional 52-card deck of playing cards has clubs, spades, diamonds, and hearts; this tarot deck has Wands, Cups, Swords, and Pentacles. Each suit has its Court cards—a King, Queen, Knight, and Page—and what are referred to as the pip cards—10, 9, 8, 7, 6, 5, 4, 3, 2, and Ace.

My quest for a deeper understanding of the cards began with an early-morning drive to upstate New York to meet with Rachel Pollack. Rachel is a Tarot Grand Master and wrote the book *78 Degrees of Wisdom*, in 1980, which is considered by many to be the bible of tarot. I had interviewed Rachel before over the phone, but this was the first time I met her in person.

I got to Rachel's house mid-morning and was greeted by Rachel; her friend Zoe Matoff, who is also a skilled tarot reader; and her dog, Wonder Girl. We sat down at Rachel's dining room table to tea and tarot. On the wall behind Rachel, I recognized a framed print of the Four of Stones from her Shining Tribe Tarot deck—a deck she developed and drew herself. The images were inspired by tribal and prehistoric art. Beyond her windows laid the woods of Upstate New York.

Pollack has been reading tarot cards for more than 30 years and has written more than a dozen books on the subject. We talked about her first introduction to the cards.

"I was teaching English at the State University of New York in 1970," Pollack said. "One of the teachers didn't have a car and it was very cold, so she said she'd read my tarot cards if I gave her a ride home. At that point, I had only heard of the tarot through a poem called "The Wasteland" by T.S. Elliot. I knew nothing about them. She did a reading for me and I re-member nothing of the reading, but I remember how completely struck I was by the cards and I thought, *Well, I have to have this.*"

"Is that when you picked up your first deck?" I asked.

"At that time, tarot cards were quite rare—it was really hard to find them. I did a lot of searching around and I finally found them in Montreal in some little tiny shop."

Pollack first began reading the cards for herself and for her friends, and her interest grew. She explained how most books up to that point were really about simplistic interpretations of each specific card. She said, "It used to be that people would just have formulas. They'd say, 'The Six of Swords means you're going to take a trip.' Today we're more likely to look at the picture and say 'Who are these people in this boat? What's this about? What are they doing? Where are they going?' and then apply that to the person's life."

People come to tarot cards with questions about almost anything, but certain questions come up more often than others for tarot readers. Questions about love, careers, friendships, family life, and health are the most popular. The person asking the questions of tarot is called the *querent*. When you're reading for yourself, you're both the querent and the reader.

In my own experiments with tarot, I've learned on the most basic level that they can be a completely objective and seemingly random way to examine an issue. For example, back in May of 2003, the first time I interviewed Rachel, she walked me through my first reading for myself. I was using her Shining Tribe Tarot deck in which the Wands, Cups, Swords, and Pentacles have been changed to Trees, Rivers, Birds, and Stones. I did a simple three-card spread where the first card represents the past, the second the present, and the third is the future. I told her that I felt as if I was coming to a crossroad in my career—my choice was to take a chance and do what I love or stay on a specific path. I shuffled the cards, while thinking of my question, then cut the deck into three different piles. I restacked the piles so the bottom pile was now on top.

A simple three-card spread where the left card represents the past, the middle is the present, and the right card is the future.

I drew my first card, for the past—the Six of Trees. Pollack explained that this card represented confidence, a strong-willed approach to work, and not getting caught up in details—confidence producing a self-fulfilling prophecy to create success. My second card, representing the present, was the Three of Rivers. This is the card of cooperation, according to Pollack—partnerships, working in harmony, and a connection to people. My final card, for the future, was the Two of Rivers. She said this card suggested an even stronger partnership in the future. The card's design has two fish in the center that are forming almost a yin and yang, and she suggested that I adopt a wait-and-see attitude toward this future partnership.

My first tarot spread using Rachel Pollack's Shining Tribe Tarot deck.

I thought a lot about my reading and about my question. Where am I going with my career? The future card may come up suggesting that alliances could bring success. I may not have been thinking of any partnerships or alliances in regards to work before the reading, but now I'm forced to, and maybe an idea worth exploring will pop into my head. It's also possible that I was thinking of a possible alliance, and the fact that a card came up alluding to alliances may confirm what I was already considering.

At the time of this writing, it's been a year and a half since that first reading. In the meantime, I found a publisher for my first book and left my former full-time job to pursue a writing career. Was it in the cards for me? I wouldn't say that reading *directed* me—though I did start actively seeking a publisher just a few months later—but maybe the reading was a spot-on prediction. My partner, in this case, was my publisher.

Back at Rachel's dining room table, I got more to the point. "Can tarot be used for spirit communication?" I asked her.

"The real question is, Is there spirit communication?" Pollack said. "If there is, then you can certainly use the tarot for it, because the tarot is a great tool for communication." She thought for a moment, then said, "I'm sure that it can be done, and that tarot would be very good for that."

The Magician, from Rachel Pollack's Shining Tribe Tarot.

At that point, Zoe Matoff cut Rachel's Shining Tribe Tarot deck with her left hand and held up the bottom card. It was the Magician, depicting a shaman in front of a river and mountains, holding his right hand high in the air and pointing at a single flower blooming in the desert with his left hand. Pollack explained how, in her tradition of tarot, the Magician is associated with the Greek god, Hermes—god of intellect, but also a guide to dead souls.

"Wow," Rachel said, "the Magician card is reaching up into the world of Heaven and pointing to the world of Earth. It's a very specific answer to your question, because the Magician is a physical channel for spirits to come into the physical world. And Zoe cut the deck at random, so there it is. That's a *very* specific answer to your question."

Zoe was as impressed as Rachel.

So the cards say it's possible to communicate with spirits. But what about in practice? Matoff said, "My best friend lives in San Francisco. Her father had died a few months earlier, and I gave her one of my very first tarot readings. A chill came over me and I realized something; I said, 'Your father is trying to talk to you.' She had herself [the card representing herself] and her father's card [the card representing her father] crossing her, and all around her, in the Celtic Cross, were members of her family. So I said, 'I think your father wants you to know something.' I wasn't able to tell her what it was that he wanted her to know, but he was there."

I learned that the Celtic Cross is one of the most popular tarot spreads. The pattern lays out a complex web of insight for the querent.

Celtic Cross Tarot Spread

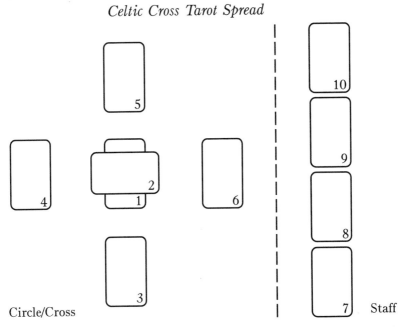

Circle/Cross   Staff

The querent focuses on an issue or question, shuffles, then cuts the deck with his or her left hand. The spread is then laid out in the order indicated on the cards in the diagram. Not only do the individual cards in this spread have meaning, but the picture and story as a whole also have a message to deliver.

Whether the messages come from within or beyond the reader, the experience is different for every tarot user. But those who make tarot an integral part of their lives feel there is something working beyond random chance. "Tarot develops your intuitive abilities," Matoff said. "Occultists from every angle say working with the tarot changes every cell in your body so you become more evolved."

Matoff isn't the only person to find magic in the cards. I also spoke with Dorothy Morrison, a Wiccan High Priestess of the Georgian Tradition and author of the book *Everyday Tarot Magic: Meditation & Spells*. She also developed the *Whimsical Tarot* with illustrator Mary Hanson-Roberts—a deck and accompanying book based on nursery rhymes and fairy tales. Morrison is a Texas girl who now lives in Maine, though she's having trouble adapting to the chillier climes. "Honey, if the God and Goddess had meant for me to live in the cold, I would have been born in the north," she said.

Morrison says she lives a magical life and sees the magical side of everything. "Everything to me is magic," she said. "Even the way the water swirls down the toilet in a clockwise direction is magic to me. When I iron clothes—I hate to iron, but usually I'm ironing out problems. So I see everything with a magical bend. Sometimes even getting a checkbook to balance is magic."

"This is true!" I said. "So how can we use tarot for magic?"

She said, "If, for example, I need courage or I need strength, what better symbol than the Ace of Swords? I might put that on my altar and meditate on that, and focus on the sword being my weapon to defend and protect."

"So there's no randomness? You go through the deck and you pull out the card that you want?"

"Exactly. Now if I'm going to use it for magic, I embed that image in my mind and take that with me so that if I get frightened, or if I feel that I'm not up to a challenge, I know that I've got that sword and I can wield it."

I asked Morrison for an example of a simple spell using tarot cards. She gave one from her book, *Everyday Tarot Magic*. She said, "It's really simple, and it doesn't take anything except the cards. This is if you need the courage to be yourself—a lot of people have trouble with that. For this, you have to understand the Hierophant [the fifth card in the Major Arcana]. The Hierophant dances to his own drummer. At one point he felt trapped by society's expectations, so now he's going to dance to his own drummer. What you do is you visualize the characteristics of the Hierophant—you visualize yourself embracing those. And you learn to dance to your own drummer and not give a damn what other people think of you. And you carry that card with you as a charm. I know this stuff sounds too simple to work, I understand that, but believe it or not, it does work."

Carrying a card with you actually didn't sound that strange to me, considering I've carried the ace of hearts and ace of spades from a traditional deck of playing cards in my wallet for many years. The cards are there to remind me that I'm a gambler and to take a chance. Plus, any gambler will tell you that two aces in the hole is a significant foundation to lean your bet on. I guess I've been practicing magic and didn't even know it.

Tarot cards have deeper meaning because we give them deeper meaning. Our belief in the meaning gives the cards their power. To understand more about the tarot market, I spoke to Stuart R. Kaplan.

Kaplan has played a significant role in bringing tarot to the level where it is today. He is the founder and Chairman of US Games Systems, Inc. in Stamford, Connecticut, and has the world's largest collection of tarot decks—numbering in the thousands—and some individual cards in his collection date back to the mid-15th century and are worth a fortune. If you haven't heard of US Games, next time you're in a New Age store or bookstore that carries tarot decks, pick up any box of tarot cards and see whose logo/brand name is on the box. It is more than likely that you'll pick up a deck either produced or distributed by US Games; the company has an overwhelming majority of tarot market share.

The back of Kaplan's business card has the image of the Fool (the zero card in the Major Arcana), and US Games's logo is a silhouette of the Fool. I asked Kaplan where that came from. "I was born April first," he said. "That's probably one of the main reasons. And I relate to the Fool because the Fool is willing to step out and do new things, and I left Wall Street to do this."

Obviously not a fool, because his risk paid off in a very big way, Kaplan had worked on Wall Street for years, but his life changed when he was at the Nuremberg Toy Fair in Germany in 1968. He happened upon a Swiss tarot deck that he became enamored with, brought the deck home, and had them reproduced. His initial printing of 100 decks sold out in a New York minute. By the end of the first year, he had sold 200,000 decks. Tarot became a hobby-turned-side-business for the next decade until 1978, when he left Wall Street to pursue tarot research, publishing, and marketing as a full-time business. Kaplan is quick to say he doesn't use tarot for fortune telling, nor does he have his cards read. He's a great admirer of the artwork and the history.

Kaplan has authored several books on tarot, including three volumes of his *Encyclopedia of Tarot*, of which he's about to publish the fourth.

US Games has published hundreds of new tarot decks over their years of operation. A flip through their current catalog shows decks as kid-friendly as the Gummy Bear Tarot, a deck by Dietmar Bittrich that shows the popular candy as cartoons in classic Rider-Waite poses throughout the deck; culturally diverse decks such as the Royal Thai Tarot, by Sungkom Horhain, with its Thai-influenced artwork; and even the trendy The Lord of the Rings Tarot deck and card game, by Terry Donaldson, Peter Pracowink, and Mike Fitzgerald, featuring characters from the popular J.R.R. Tolkien books that were made into the hugely successful movie trilogy. And of course, they also publish the Rider-Waite deck, which outsells every other deck 500 to one.

In the last 10 years, US Games has diversified its product line to include more card games, playing cards, strategy cards, leadership cards, and natural world cards, but tarot still represents a little more than half of the company's business.

"How has the use of tarot evolved over the last 30 years?" I asked.

"In the 1970s, it was very esoteric—occult, fortune telling, that kind of thing," Kaplan said. "It has definitely changed, whereas today its collectors want it because of its imagery. People like the artwork, people use it for meditation, and people do still use it for fortune telling. People are challenged by not only the artwork, but the symbolism. It's a much broader interest in tarot today than what was in the 70s."

"What mark do you hope to leave on tarot?"

Kaplan said, "Having made it available, and having separated fantasy from fact in the *Encyclopedias*. We've tried to really find out what it's all about, when did it start, why did it start, who might have started it—which is why we really do a lot of research on the early history: the Viscontis, the Sforzas, the Corleones, Northern Italy, and Milan. People can't possibly have the collection that we have, because it's so enormous in terms of quantity. So the idea was to do encyclopedias and try to reproduce the cards so that people can see all the differences in the artwork."

We talked more about the changing face of tarot over the centuries. For example, the Carey pack, which was produced in 1791, featured the Grandmother and Grandfather instead of the Empress and the Emperor, because of the strong antiroyalist feelings leading up to the French revolution.

Tarot artwork has always been a mirror of what was happening in society. Tarot's imagery has also been a place to depict mythic legends, religious lore, and other sacred ideas. There are a surprising number of Christians who are beginning to use tarot to explore their own faith. Christians believe many of the cards depict (or at least *could* depict) parts of Biblical scripture. For example, the Tower in the Major Arcana shows a structure reaching into the clouds and being struck by lightning; it's on fire and crumbling, and two people are falling from the top— some believe this relates directly to the Tower of Babel. The Strength card, also in the Major Arcana, depicts a woman holding the upper and lower jaws of a lion. Could this be from the Old Testament story (Judges 14: 5–9) where Samson killed the lion with his bare hands? The Last Judgment card is pretty self-explanatory, as is the Devil. There are many other cards throughout the deck that could be interpreted as biblically influenced, and therein lies part of tarot's charm—it can adapt and be adapted to suit both sacred and secular purposes.

Those Christians using tarot to explore their faith have certainly raised the feathers of many of their fellow parishioners who feel tarot is a tool of the occult and is specifically warned against in the book of Deuteronomy. Playing cards were, in fact, warned against by the Church in the 15th and 16th centuries as instruments of evil, but the tarot was exempt from this warning. It was exempt because the Church was trying to stop the masses from gambling—something they were doing with the less-expensive, 52-card decks, not something they were doing with tarot.

In the late 1700s, tarot was used for *cartomancy* (telling fortunes with cards) by some and has since given the cards their occult reputation. Ironically, modern 52-card decks are no longer seen as evil in the general Christian community, though people do still gamble with them and some also use these decks for fortune telling. Part of tarot's charm for many is its mystical reputation and the allegorical imagery inscribed on its cards.

If a single drawing or painting is the artist's equivalent of a sprint, then designing a tarot deck is a marathon—according to renowned tarot artist, Kris Waldherr. Waldherr is the artist behind The Goddess Tarot, a deck that has sold more than 200,000 copies, and The Lover's Path Tarot (released in the fall of 2004).

Waldherr works in different mediums, depending on the project; The Goddess Tarot was created in watercolor and colored pencil.

Designing a tarot deck requires a minimum of 78 images, though usually it amounts to 80 with the two extras —one card that serves as an introduction to the

Card XVII—The Star of the Major Arcana from Kris Waldherr's The Goddess Tarot deck.

deck and a card to give credit to the artists/developers of the deck.

"With such a big undertaking, do you wait for the muse to hit before you begin?" I asked.

"I think you have to invite the muse," Waldherr said. "When you've been working, like I have for the past 20 years, as a professional artist, you realize that you have a relationship with the muse. It's like you do the work and hopefully they show up."

"So why create a new tarot deck? What sparked that for you?" I asked.

The Nine of Arrows from Kris Waldherr's The Lover's Path Tarot deck.

"The Goddess Tarot was an unusual situation in that I had a lot of the art already completed, because it was taken from a book I had done called the *Book of Goddesses*. The funny thing is that I've always been interested in the tarot. I sort of sat down one day and realized that a lot of the goddesses seemed to correspond to what would be considered the archetypes of the Major Arcana."

Waldherr had worked with tarot for many years, and having not found the kind of deck that really spoke to and inspired her, she decided to create it. This is a common story I've heard from people who have designed their own decks—they couldn't find one that worked for them perfectly, so they made one.

From looking through her Goddess deck, I could see a lot of similarities in terms of the figures, positions, and the general layout of the cards to the Rider-Waite deck. I asked if she was inspired to follow Rider-Waite in her own creation. She said, "I did to a certain extent, because I think it's too much to expect people to learn entirely different systems every time they work with a new tarot deck. I like my decks to be very accessible in that way. I hate to say that it's [Rider-Waite] the standard, but it *is* sort of the standard. What I try to do is bring something new to it."

For Waldherr, the undertaking is much bigger than just creating 80 stunning images; it's actually a big responsibility for the creator. "It's a responsibility because there's an awareness that a lot of people are going to be using this to try and transform their lives. I get letters from women who use the Goddess Tarot; one woman said she left her husband, who was being abusive to her, and my deck sort of helped her to access that part of herself that made her stronger. I don't think there's any glorified thing that I did, I think it was already within her, but if I can create a tool that helps her access that, that makes me feel really good."

Good art stirs us and forces us to explore our own emotions, thoughts, and ideas about various subjects. Visual art is itself a symbol that is open to our interpretations. But how can we connect with spirits through these cards? Or maybe a more appropriate question would be How can spirits connect with us through the cards? I have repeatedly heard from tarot readers that tarot won't work with someone who is unwilling. Meaning, if you wanted information on me, and I wasn't there or didn't consent to you using the cards to get that information, it simply wouldn't work. I've heard this from tarot readers with a more esoteric view, as well as those who take more of a pragmatic approach to readings. So how do we reach across to spirits and invite them to communicate through the tarot?

One way is actually quite literal, though not for everyone. Holly Gotcher is someone I've known for a few years now because she's a regular on Ghostvillage.com. She's been reading cards for 25 years. Gotcher grew up in New Jersey, but learned the cards during visits to her grandmother's house in Scarsdale, New York. She currently lives in Dallas, Texas, and still reads for people, though she never charges and prefers to read for people she doesn't know that well. "I hate when my family or close friends ask me to do a reading for them," Gotcher said. "I'm uncomfortable with it. If you are my best friend, I know everything that's going on. So I read for strangers."

Holly is also psychic and says she can see spirits. She has offered to read for people while traveling for business for her IT career. She said in nine or 10 of those readings throughout those 25 years, a spirit has walked up to stand near the querent. "What I do at that point is tell the person I'm doing the reading for that they do, in fact, have somebody behind them," Gotcher said. "And I describe the person [spirit] if they weren't communicating directly to me."

"So you can tell the spirit wants to communicate, but it can't simply speak to you?" I asked.

"Exactly. At that point, the reading becomes the spirit's reading. I make it clear to them [the spirit] that if they have exerted the energy that I know it takes to appear, now, while this querent is here with me, then they need to tell the querent something, and they need to tell me with the cards, so I can give the message."

Over the course of our conversation, Gotcher regularly referred to the spirit as "person," something that was at first confusing to me, but it soon became obvious that this is simply how she views the spirit—it's a person, just like the querent, just like her, just like me. This person happens to be in spirit form.

Gotcher uses tarot for spirit communication when the spirit can't get a message across any other way. She explained how she fans out the cards face up so everyone can see a little bit of each card in the deck. She explains to the querent and the spirit (though mostly to the spirit) that she is going to move her hand over the cards and they need to indicate when they want her to stop. She'll choose three cards this way for the reading in order to get the message.

She keeps a journal of her readings, so she was able to share some specifics with me on some of her more profound communication sessions. In the first case, Gotcher was reading for a woman, and a female spirit showed up behind the querent and began lovingly petting her shoulder and neck. The querent couldn't feel anything, but Holly saw it happening and described what the spirit looked like and what she was doing. The querent identified the spirit as her mother who had passed away six months earlier.

Gotcher said, "We came up with the Page of Swords in an upright position, the King of Swords reversed, and then the Two of Cups. I could see where this was going right away, and I explained to her that the Page of Swords in an upright position is trying to tell you that there is more than meets the eye. There are things that other people see and you don't see it yet. The second card was the King of Swords. He was reversed, however, so this is a *really* strong man who is more than a little angry. He has an awful lot of power, and he's very strong; the downside is he's really cruel and really insensitive. The third card, the Two of Cups, is a card of friendship. I read these cards across, and I spoke to her and her mother at the same time, and I said, 'I believe what we're being told here is that she needs you to make peace with your father. Because you haven't had any peace with him even throughout her death.'"

The querent cried. This was the reason she wanted a reading in the first place, to explore trying to make amends with her father, with whom she was estranged. The answer came from the cards, but more importantly, this querent believed the answer came for her own mother who had visited in spirit.

The second reading Gotcher told me about was even more profound, because the message turned out to be a warning that would be proven later by a doctor. This reading may have saved a life.

She said, "Going back about 15 years, I was doing a reading, and [the spirit of] a young man showed up behind the young lady that I was reading for."

"What did you do at that point?" I asked.

"I asked him to join us. I said to him, 'I do see you, and is there something that you would like me to tell her?' and he nodded yes. I said, 'You can tell me what you want to tell.' There was a lot of activity with his hands and a lot of eye contact, but a lot of it is through imagery, and these cards could not be any better for that purpose."

"How does a spirit know the meaning of the card?" I asked. "I'm not sure I could build a reading right now, given my limited understanding."

"My thought has always been that the spirits feel the cards through me," Gotcher said. "The first time I did this, I had the cards upside down for some reason and was asked to turn them over by the spirit, which I did. As I scanned each card, the spirit watched me intently and told me when to stop. I don't think they gain the skill to use the cards after death, but I do find that often spirits are quite intuitive and use any symbols they may perceive as a way of communication."

Gotcher described this male spirit to the querent and found out this was the querent's brother. This spirit was frustrated at being recognized but not being able to get his message across. So she fanned the tarot cards out and explained how she would draw three cards at the spirit's direction.

"I ran my fingers over the cards until I reached the Page of Pentacles reversed—not a good card. This is the first one we stopped at. Next, I came up with two Queens, both upright. Normally I'll do a three-card reading in a situation like this, but after the two Queens he was very agitated that I continue, and so I did, and I got both of the other Queens. So we had the first Page of Pentacles surrounded by four Queens. This is really interesting to me because this is pretty unusual. I know the Page of Pentacles reversed is not good news and often bodes of an illness. You need to read the surrounding cards to get the whole picture. Being surrounded by four females, I thought that her problem lied there—in female anatomy problems. So I told her that she needed to go to a gynecologist and have a complete checkup, because she had a messenger here carrying bad news, most likely of illness. I said to her, 'I think this is the best your brother can do to direct us to where the problem is and you need to go.'

"I kept in touch with this woman, and she did go [to the doctor] within two weeks because she was so shaken by this reading. And, in fact, she had breast cancer. She had a mastectomy, and she told me that her prognosis was excellent. I like to think that, between her brother and me, we got her there in time to take care of what she needed to do."

Holly's husband, Dave Gotcher, also reads cards and has his own way of spirit communication through tarot cards. Before beginning, he asks if there are any spirits in the room and for their help in guiding his reading to be as accurate and honest as possible. He said, "When I do a one-card reading, I ribbon-fan the cards face down, as opposed to Holly's face up, and run my hand from left to right until I 'feel' the pull of the card, effectively drawing it blind. Then I continue down the rest of the fan to make sure no other cards are needing to be seen." Dave then interprets the message based on that one card, or multiple cards if that's the case.

After taking into account all of the things I had learned, it was time for me to give it a try on my own. I don't consider myself psychic or even sensitive, so I needed to come up with a question/scenario that could be answered with the cards and at least give the impression of being influenced by a spirit or spirits.

Of all my relatives who have passed on, I feel the closest to my maternal grandfather. I sat shuffling my Rider-Waite tarot deck for a few minutes. The act of shuffling almost became a type of meditation in and of itself. I was shuffling but not thinking about the cards; I was thinking about my grandfather. He died in 2001, and I've held on to the notion that he's been near me throughout my life since.

I closed my eyes and asked in a whisper whether, if he was still near, he could communicate with me through these cards—all the while shuffling. I asked him if he was still watching over me.

I set the deck down on my desk and cut it with my left hand. I then drew three cards. The cards that came up were, from left to right: the Nine of Swords, reversed (or upside-down); the Three of Swords; and the Ace of Wands, also reversed.

The Nine of Swords featured a gray-haired old man sitting up in bed and holding his face as though he's crying. Above him on the wall are nine swords. The Three of Swords features a valentine heart floating in the clouds and being pierced by three swords. The Ace of Wands shows a hand coming out of a cloud and holding a stick with a few leaves falling off of it.

The heart floating in the clouds in the middle card was what drew most of my attention because it seemed ethereal in a way.

I don't know why, but for me, it seemed to represent my grandfather. The instruction pamphlet that accompanies the deck (which happens to be written by Stuart Kaplan) tells a different story.

According to the instructions, the divinatory meaning of the Nine of Swords reversed is "Imprisonment, doubt, suspicion, reasonable fear, shame." The Three of Swords: "Removal, absence, delay, division, rupture, dispersion, and all that the design signifies naturally." Finally, the Ace of Wands reversed: "Fall, decadence, ruin, perdition, to perish, also—clouded joy." So for the most part, this is a rather bleak reading, by the book.

I posted the results of my spread to Ghostvillage.com and asked some tarot readers for their interpretation of the cards. At first, I simply posted the results and didn't mention anything about the nature of my question.

Here are three interesting analyses of the spread from three different members:

First Interpretation:

"The first card is an end of doubt, the second is the end of an affair of the heart, and the third is an unrealized goal or sterility," said one of my readers, based on her own intution and Robin Wood's The Robin Wood Tarot deck and book that she consults as a guide to meaning.

Second Interpretation:

"The Nine of Swords, reversed: a period of anxiety has recently been lifted from you. Something was causing you a lot of stress and sleepless nights. That sphere of influence is now past, but driving you on to further goals.

"The Three of Swords: right now you're uncomfortably separated from your daily routine. However, this change was needed in order for you to move forward. This card also heralds a period when any self-delusion will fall away and the true nature of your situation will come to you with more gravity.

"The Ace of Wands, reversed: a new idea that has not yet materialized but one that may well define your future more than past events in your life. Potential, but within the realm of a creative venture that has already manifested. Shaky faith in your own abilities, uncertainty where to go next. Fear of exposing your inner self to the outside world."

This reader based her interpretation on her own lifelong experience working with the cards and the book that accompanies *The Mythic Tarot* by Juliet Sherman-Burke and Liz Greene.

Third Interpretation:

"Time is healing, and you will have gained strength of character from the experience you have been through. The loss that is currently present in your life is strong—it could be a result of an argument or a separation. The surrounding cards generally explain where the sorrow is coming from. You're missing something and must take time to regroup."

Between the Rider-Waite booklet's definition of the cards and the three interpretations offered online, I think my reading was pretty inconclusive. When I saw the three cards, I wasn't overwhelmed with the sense of a specific answer, but maybe I didn't ask the right question, or maybe I don't yet understand the dialect being spoken through the cards.

There is a language to tarot, and to use it properly, that language needs to be learned. Learning takes time and study. By using the cards repeatedly, one learns the meaning by sight, but also learns to look at the bigger picture of each spread. Intuition is a vital part of tarot reading. Storytelling is also part of tarot—seeing the images line up or form a pattern and deciding what may have brought these "characters" to this point. Tarot begs us to tell the story of each card and each spread and apply it to our own life. Its imagery and meaning will be up to each querent to interpret and understand. It's also up to each querent whether to believe the cards are being affected by a spirit or spirits or if it's simply luck of the draw.

"Spirit photography is an aided type of mediumship—using the camera to communicate with spirits, or rather, using the camera to let spirits communicate with you. When, how, or why the spirits choose to appear or make contact is of their doing."

Spirit Photography

Have you ever looked at a photograph of yourself and said, "I don't even think that looks like me"? That's because it isn't you. A photograph is a two-dimensional representation of a three-dimensional object. So your features are flattened into the background of whatever you're standing in front of. I learned this in college when I took a photography course. This by no means makes me a photography expert, but I do know how to develop and print my own film, and I'm good enough with photo manipulation programs such as Adobe Photoshop to be able to create a convincing picture of the Pope chugging beer at a bowling alley.

Because I have a basic understanding of photography, I'm skeptical about many alleged "spirit photographs." Fingers in front of the lens, double exposures, and lens flares are just some of the many photographic miscues that often get labeled as supernatural. But assuming the person who took the photo wasn't trying to deceive, some spirit photography images have certainly made me say, "Hmmm." And a very select few have even made me say, "Wow!"

Over the years, many people have sent me their samples of spirit photos. I'm always apprehensive to comment on them because there usually is no right answer. For example, someone might send in a picture and say, "Check out the flesh-colored, glowing ghost on the right edge of this picture." If I write back, "That looks like you may have had one of your fingers in front of the lens," I've been known to get angry replies to the effect that I'm being too skeptical or insensitive and questioning why I can't see that the fleshy blob is their beloved Uncle Bucky, who passed away last year. I've learned that the picture *is* proof to the person who took it. For the photographer, it's irrefutable evidence of an afterlife that he or she can reference for as long as the photo is in existence. This parallels the very nature of spirituality—it's an individual experience. No two ideas of spirituality are the same, and one man's ghost is another man's blurred finger. To understand, you may need to take one of these pictures for yourself.

The question that repeatedly comes up in regard to spirit photography is: Can a camera take a picture of something you didn't see with your naked eye? It's the question that the entire concept of spirit photography hinges on.

Spirit photography got its start soon after the camera did. There are many important dates and great minds whose works led up to the development of the camera. For example, between 1664 and 1666, Isaac Newton discovered, through work with prisms, how white light is broken into a spectrum of colors (red, orange, yellow, green, blue, indigo, violet, and all of the shades in between). In 1727, Johann Heinrich Schulze found that the chemical silver nitrate darkened when exposed to light. In 1814, Joseph Nicéphore Niépce made the first photographic image with his "camera obscura," but the process needed a lot of work— the image needed up to eight hours of exposure to light and it wasn't permanent. Arguably marking the most significant year for the camera, in 1837, Louis-Jacques-Mandé Daguerre, a French-born painter, came up with a device and development method that needed only 30 minutes of light exposure and didn't fade. He named his camera after himself, the *daguerreotype*.

Daguerre sold the rights to this new device to the French government in 1839. On August 19, 1839, the invention was officially announced at a French Academy of Sciences meeting in Paris, and from there, photography spread throughout the world. There were more advances and improvements to the camera in the coming decades, such as William Henry Talbot's new Calotype in 1841, which was the first to use a negative-positive process that made producing multiple copies of a picture possible. More breakthroughs came every few years as inventors redesigned or improved upon existing processes and products.

During all of this photographic technology development, we also had the birth of the Spiritualist movement in 1848. Spiritualists were quick to adopt and adapt technology because part of their belief system is that spirits and spirit communication can be proved. Could this new camera have been the device to capture that proof?

By 1855, just 16 years after the daguerreotype became widely available, people began reporting the capture of supernatural phenomena on their photographs. In this letter printed in the March 31, 1855 issue of the New York-based *Spiritual Telegraph* newspaper—a publication by and for the Spiritualist community—William H. Hutchings of New Orleans, Louisiana, describes a daguerreotype photo he took on February 8, 1855:

> A most wonderful spiritual manifestation occurred in my daguerreotype saloon about 11 or 12 o'clock yesterday forenoon. I was taking a likeness of my mother-in-law, Mrs. Moore, of Philadelphia, with my seventh son, an infant just two months old, in her arms, and after three unsuccessful trials in consequence of the babe's moving, I prepared a plate for a fourth trial; and having learned by two year's experience that we are dependent upon the Lord for all things, I sought success through prayer (let the skeptic sneer), and then took an impression in a *single second*—my usual time for taking an impression of an infant. I found a beautiful, sharp, distinct picture of the babe and his grandmother, and upon the arm of the babe a bright ray of golden-colored spiritual light, which extended from an angle of ten degrees south of the zenith, alongside of the grandmother's head, descending upon the arm of the babe. I send you by mail a copy of the picture, which I trust you

will *retain in your own hands,* as there are many copies of this to be taken, I am impressed. Now, that such a ray of light can be produced in such a picture by natural appliances of art, I do not for one moment believe. The ray, you will perceive, is of almost equal width through the entire length, and in this it differs from natural rays of light entirely. Now let the scientific world solve the problem by natural philosophy if they can! After a close examination of all the circumstances of the case, endeavoring to account for this wonderful phenomenon, I was about concluding that it was an accident, and thus unaccountable; but the Spirit immediately told me it was a spiritual ray, from an angel of light—one of my own children.

In 1862, spirit photography took a turn toward the mainstream. An engraver named William H. Mumler in Boston took a self-portrait, and when he developed the picture, there was another semitransparent, recognizably human figure in the picture with him.

Mumler's wife was herself a psychic medium and involved with the Spiritualist movement. Perhaps her beliefs influenced her husband? Perhaps her husband saw an opportunity? Once word of Mumler's spirit photograph spread, he claimed his own medium abilities and began to charge $10 per portrait for "guaranteed results." This was during a time when normal photographic portraits cost less than 50 cents.

One of Mumler's most renowned customers was Mary Todd Lincoln, the widow of assassinated president Abraham Lincoln. She had long believed in the power of mediums and immediately sought to contact her deceased husband. Mumler's portrait of Mary Todd featured a tall, bearded man standing over her.

Mumler's photographs and business practice were investigated within two years of starting up. Many of the "spirits" in the photographs were actually living residents of Boston who had been paid to pose for these sessions. Mumler was exposed as a fraud, and he destroyed most of his images and plates in a rage. The Mumlers moved from Boston to New York to try to start the business again, but he was quickly arrested and again charged with fraud.

To understand spirit photography, and thus spirit communication with a camera, I wanted to start at the very beginning of the equation—what there is to see and how we see it. I spoke with Dr. Lawrence K. Fox, an ophthalmologist with Central New York Eye Center in Fishkill, New York. First, we talked about what we can and cannot see in the electromagnetic spectrum.

The electromagnetic spectrum starts at the low end with radio waves, which have the longest wavelengths. Next come microwaves, then infrared, then the visible part of the spectrum that we can see, which consists of shades of red, orange, yellow, green, blue, indigo, and violet. Next comes ultraviolet; then x-rays; and finally gamma rays, at the other end of the spectrum, with the shortest waves.

We can only see a tiny fraction of the electromagnetic spectrum—the part we can see is appropriately called the visible spectrum. To give you an idea of how small this part of the spectrum is, try this analogy: If you were standing on a football field, and the end zone on your left represented radio waves (the longest), and the end zone on your right represented gamma rays (the shortest), the visible spectrum would comprise about a 2-foot strip of that 100-yard field and would be located just past midfield, favoring the gamma side.

There is activity going on all over our football field, but we can only see a 2-foot strip without the aid of special equipment. There are many theories that spirits utilize electromagnetic energy to manifest and materialize. If this is true, then perhaps they normally operate in other parts of the spectrum and occasionally make an appearance in the narrow band that we can see?

I've certainly heard many accounts of animals who seem enthralled with some "invisible presence." Some people claim it as evidence that their animals see a spirit that we can't. Science actually supports this idea in a way, because some animals and insects can see shorter and sometimes longer wavelengths than humans—something that increases their field of vision slightly. Maybe your dog or cat really is onto something when it becomes preoccupied with blank space in the corner of your living room.

But back to the human eye. Knowing what there is to see, I asked Dr. Fox how our eyes work. "There are optics within the eye," he said. "The cornea is the front part of the eye, and that does most of the focusing. Then behind the iris, the brown or blue part of one's eyes, there's a lens that takes care of the remaining part of the focusing. Ideally, light comes in, hits those two optical elements, and is focused exactly on the retina, which is the inner lining of the back part of the eye."

"So what happens when the light comes in?" I asked.

"The retina has a lot of different types of cells, but the cells that you'd be concerned with are called *photo receptors*. They take light energy, transform it into chemical and then electrical energy, which then goes to the optic nerve—which is like a trunk of nerves—and then into the brain. The brain interprets this electrical energy as what we perceive as sight."

Not too surprisingly, a camera is very similar to the eye. For help with cameras and photography, I spoke with Ken Milburn, a photographer based in San Francisco, California, with more than 50 years of experience. Milburn is also the author of *Digital Photography: 99 Easy Tips to Make You Look Like a Pro* and *The Digital Photography Bible*, among 18 other books on photography and image manipulation.

We first talked about how cameras work. Film cameras are actually very simple and are comprised of only three pieces: a lens (the optical piece), some film (the chemical piece), and the camera body (the mechanical piece).

As we discussed earlier, visible light travels at different wavelengths, depending on the color. The lens's job is to slow the light down and bend it, aiming it at a specific point inside the back of the camera. This is why the lens is typically convex, or bulging outward on a camera. With the light bent and pinpointed inside the camera, the mechanics are now ready to do their part. When you push the shutter release button, the mechanical part of the camera opens a tiny window called the *aperture* behind the lens for a specific amount of time (this depends on your shutter speed settings but is typically a fraction of a second). This allows the bent light to be burned onto the film—the chemical part of the equation.

This is an intentionally over-simplified description of how all film cameras work, from your disposable point-and-shoot to the $5,000 camera on the sideline of a professional football game. It's important to understand these basics so we know what can go wrong.

"Film is very susceptible to getting either chemically polluted or aged over time in such a way that strange things appear to be on the film that have nothing to do with anything except the hand of God," Milburn said. "And I don't mean in the ghostly kind of way. It's also very susceptible to dirt and dust and little particles of anything."

We talked about how to handle and control film. Professional photographers tend to buy their film in batches that have been tested by the film manufacturer. Additionally, the film is always stored in a controlled environment, such as a refrigerator, and never gets to be more than a few months old. Old film or film that is exposed to heat and/or extreme cold can have altered chemicals that cause anomalies and distortions in the pictures. Moreover, with high-volume photo development houses, such as Wal-Mart or your local pharmacy, many times the chemicals can become contaminated and also cause strange results in pictures.

When talking about cameras, it soon becomes obvious that Milburn is a strong advocate of digital photography (as if his author credits weren't enough). In listening to his reasons for going digital, I certainly understand.

"It's a lot harder to get dirt on a digital image because the CCD [Charge Coupled Device]—the light-sensitive device that records the picture—is sealed up." So camera users aren't opening and closing the film compartment again and again, introducing dirt and dust where the film will be.

Among paranormal investigators, the type of camera to use is a polarizing argument. The argument for film is that you have the negative to examine and you can prove you didn't tamper with the image. On the negative you can look for signs of light leaks from the camera or chemical spills that may have been introduced in processing. But there are some compelling reasons to go digital as well (besides the obvious cost savings and instant gratification).

I asked Milburn, "Can a digital camera see more than the human eye can?"

"A digital camera not only can, but *will* see more than your eye. Whether or not you ever see what the camera saw is a wholly different question.

"One of the strange characteristics of digital is that the collection of image sensors can record a much broader range of tonal values than the human eye can see. The software in the camera interprets what the camera captured. Most people shoot JPEG, not RAW files, so the camera decides what to do with all of that raw information—what it should keep and what it should throw away. The camera might record some of the spectrums of light beyond the visible spectrum because it is sensitive to infrared and ultraviolet. The camera software may decide to keep something from the infrared or ultraviolet part of the spectrum for whatever reason—its algorithms might decide it's bright enough, or it's going to overcorrect for green because there's too much green in the picture, and that sort of thing."

I was intrigued by this notion. There are some people who only shoot infrared cameras when searching for the presence of a spirit. If spirits are "living" outside the visible spectrum most of the time, then the digital camera will offer us a slightly broader view within the electromagnetic spectrum—a somewhat wider view of our football field, if you will.

"Digital cameras all have infrared filters on them that are more or less effective according to the camera manufacturer's proclivity for being politically correct—because truly infrared can take people's clothes off," Milburn said.

Two years ago, Sony had to take one of its camcorders off the market because its night vision capability, when used in the daytime, could in fact see through some clothes. There are many digital camera cell phones that reportedly have the same problem (or feature, depending on your perspective).

I sent Milburn about a dozen images from my vast collection of anomalous photos taken by me and others who submitted their pictures to Ghostvillage.com. Granted, he did not get to see any of the original files or negatives, and we had to operate under the assumption that the people who took the pictures were not trying to intentionally trick anybody. I started by showing him some of my many examples of orbs.

"Lens flare," he said without any hesitation. Even when the orbs were positioned in seemingly random places around a photo, he explained how lens flare could still be the cause. "The lenses in most digital cameras have four to nine elements," Milburn said. "That's four to nine separate lenses that are glued together to correct for various types of aberrations. So each one of those surfaces is capable of taking up a reflection and recording it. It doesn't necessarily have to be some bright light that you can see inside the frame, either. It could be something that is off to the side that just happens to hit the front of the lens and then reflects on the elements of the lens. Lens flare can even look like a ball in motion because of the multiple lenses."

When I got my first digital camera back in 2000, it was an Olympus 1.3 megapixel camera and I carried it with me any time I went to visit family, friends, or allegedly haunted places. I was regularly capturing orbs in my images, and I sent some of these photos to Olympus and asked them what they were. Their explanation was that the flash, combined with ever-improving imaging technology, was causing the cameras to pick up dust particles and droplets of moisture in the air and cast a glowing ball around them. Critics of the orb phenomenon make the argument that, while general consumer cameras have gone down in cost and increased in quality, the camera's decrease in physical size means the flash is dangerously close to the lens. In other words, the flash fires and bounces off of every possible shining surface as the camera opens and closes its shutter to capture the image. The flash seems to be the repeated culprit.

Another argument for the support of lens flare isn't only the location of the flash but its very nature. The flash travels at the speed of light, or 186,000 miles per second. Considering that your average point-and-shoot camera has a shutter speed of 1/125 of a second, the light from the flash has the opportunity to travel 1,488 miles during the time your shutter is open.

Stay with me here.... If you're in a 20-foot by 20-foot room; the light from your flash has traveled roughly 1,488 miles within that room and has bounced off of every reflective, shiny, or moist surface; then the light gets bounced, reflected, and refracted over four to nine separate lenses, the likelihood of lens flare in any part of the image seems obvious.

One reason orbs can't be completely discounted, however, is that I've spoken to many witnesses who claim to have seen orbs with their naked eye. If they had a camera at that moment, they could have taken a picture of the phenomenon.

And what about how quickly our brains can process visual information? Your average blockbuster Hollywood movies run at 24 frames per second, meaning that every second of film that you watch consists of 24 pictures, each slightly different than the last. The human eye can't discern much past 30 frames per second. My old, fully manual Pentax K1000 35mm camera has a dial to set shutter speeds. The fastest shutter speed on this camera is 1/1000 of a second, followed by 1/500, 1/250, 1/125, 1/60, 1/30, 1/15, 1/8, 1/4, 1/2, 1, and one setting that holds the shutter open as long as the button is depressed. You'll notice that most of the shutter speeds are faster than 1/30 of a second. In fact, having taken many pictures with this camera, at 1/30 of a second, you'd better have either a tripod for your camera or a very steady hand, because your pictures can come out blurry with the slightest movement. Typical point-and-shoot cameras operate roughly four times faster than the human eye can discern.

This example can translate into real life as well. You've heard the expression "the hand is quicker than the eye." Hold this book with one hand and, with your free hand, hold up one finger and pass it between your eyes and the books as fast as you can. You'll find that you can easily keep reading because your finger is practically transparent, given the speed at which it is moving.

If a glowing ball, which I'll call a "thing" for the sake of some healthy skepticism, just passed between you and this book right now and that "thing" is even smaller than your finger and moving even faster, you would have never seen it. It simply would be moving too rapidly. But if you aimed your camera at the book, you would capture that "thing" in the photo. Of course the next conclusion is that you'd have to be phenomenally lucky to decide to click your camera at the fraction of a second when something was passing just a foot or two in front of you. Maybe so, or maybe that "thing" or "energy" is present in a location and darting all around your field of vision. You could only see it with your eye if it stood still or slowed down considerably. If a camera takes a picture of an entire room, it may just catch something anomalous in transit.

Granted, many paranormal investigators today dismiss orb photos in general because there are so many explanations for them that they're too inconclusive. But there are other anomalies that certainly stump even the professional photographers.

Ken Milburn and I went over several other examples I'd sent him of streaks of light energy, mists, and even some apparitions. He was able to explain how to re-create some of the images, such as using a tripod and setting the camera to a shutter speed of a few seconds, then running through the room with a flashlight, but this would be an intentional fake—not someone with a point-and-shoot camera snapping a quick picture. Assuming we weren't victims of duping, some of these photos were harder for Milburn to explain.

In the 1860s, William Mumler of Boston had faked his spirit photos in a clever but very simple way. Daguerreotype cameras needed a very long shutter speed—sometimes up to a minute or more. The subject of the photo had to remain motionless or the picture would come out blurry. With the subject sitting and facing the camera, Mumler would have one of his actors, dressed in a flowing robe, jump into the picture for 10 to 15 seconds, then jump out. The result would be a semitransparent, ghostly image. The other way to take such a picture is what is called a double exposure. Take the portrait in a very normal way, then escort the subject out of the room. Mumler could then bring his "ghost" in and open the camera's shutter again for a few seconds on the same plate, and the result would be the ghostly figure.

"I've shot lots of fashion pictures that are done that way," Milburn said. "Not to create ghosts, but because it's an interesting effect. Say you've got a 30-second exposure—which is about the longest you can keep a lens open on a digital camera; after that, the image becomes so noisy that nobody wants to keep the picture. The model poses in one place for a fairly long time, say 10 seconds, and then changes to three or four other complementary positions for maybe five seconds apiece, moving quickly in between. In the final image, you don't see anything in between;

what you see are these neat little pictures of her wearing the same dress, which are sort of ghostly in the background. It's a gorgeous effect."

In September of 2004, I stayed in a campground in Gettysburg, Pennsylvania, with some other ghost investigators. We went into the battlefields just after sundown to look for ghostly activity. It was a Saturday night and one of those last hurrahs for summer weather. In the Devil's Den battlefield, I was astounded at how many people were out there in the pitch dark trying to take spirit photos. There were older couples who looked to be in their 60s, pulling their cars over on the side of the road, rolling down their windows, and snapping pictures of the dark field in front of them. There were families with small children walking the trails and clicking pictures. Literally dozens of people were out on this one particular night—all trying to capture a supernatural souvenir from Gettysburg. This practice is growing among the masses.

Just as the supernatural experience runs across a wide spectrum of phenomena, so too do spirit photographs. There are a few definitions that are reasonably agreed upon by paranormal investigators.

Orb: A spherical-shaped, usually semitranslucent mass of energy, they can appear as small as pebbles to as large as beach balls. *Supernatural theory:* The basic shape of a spirit, the form a soul travels in.

Streak: Either an orb in motion or some perceived line of energy moving in a specific pattern. *Supernatural theory:* Spirit energy in motion.

Mist, Ectoplasm, or Spirit Matter: Smoky, sometimes swirling material that may even contain recognizable features. *Supernatural theory:* The material produced by a spirit just before or left behind just after materializing.

Vortex: A tornado-like funnel of mist/energy that is sometimes dense, sometimes semitranslucent. *Supernatural theory:* The gateway spirits use to enter and leave our physical plane.

Apparition: A form with recognizable features. Some-times a semitranslucent human or animal form, sometimes recognizable features forming from within mist or spirit matter. *Supernatural theory:* A ghost or spirit that is in some stage of materializing.

Since 2000, I've had a friend who takes some of the most consistently profound spirit photographs I've seen. His name is Jim DeCaro and he was kind enough to provide the cover photo for this book. I went to see him in his home in Connecticut one day during the summer of 2004. Jim was raised in Long Island, New York, and is a former Marine. The first time I met him, his accent and animated mannerisms seemed to contrast with his interest in the pursuit of spirit contact, but soon afterward, I realized he truly has a passion for the study.

After heading out for a quick breakfast, we went to Long Hill Cemetery in Trumbull, Connecticut. This was the cemetery where DeCaro took the cover photo, in early July of 1999, on only his second expedition into spirit photography. The cemetery opened in 1764 and is still in use to this day, as was evident by two men digging a new grave when we arrived.

DeCaro and I pulled into the cemetery to walk by some of the older headstones found on the western side. Many obelisks point skyward around Long Hill Cemetery, and many of the older headstones are adorned with old New England death heads—a cartoonish skull with bird-like wings.

A 1765 tombstone in Long Hill Cemetery in Trumbull, Connecticut, featuring a winged death head, a head-stone style popular during puritanical times. Photo by Jeff Belanger.

DeCaro talked about how he got started in spirit photography at the urging of his friend, psychic, and author, Jeffrey Wands. Wands told him to take his camera to "where the dead are."

"In the beginning, it was curiosity—like it probably is for a lot of other people," he said. "I was thinking that it's going to happen, then reality hits and you think, 'Yeah, I'm going to just take my camera and go capture a picture of a spirit. Me and everybody else, right?'"

But he did start capturing spirit material in his images within his first night of trying. What makes DeCaro's approach different than many is that this has become a truly spiritual endeavor—a means of making contact with the spirit world by using a camera. "The camera is there to substantiate what you think," he said. "What you've been through and what you've seen. It's there to document the occasion."

After leaving Long Hill Cemetery, we drove a few miles away to the town of Easton. We were heading to Union Cemetery, the place where DeCaro took his first spirit photographs. I grew up just two towns away from Easton in Newtown, Connecticut, so I had heard the legends of "The White Lady of Easton." The White Lady has been spotted all around Union Cemetery and along Sport Hill Road and Route 59, which intersect at the cemetery.

Similar to the cemetery in Trumbull, Union also has head-stones dating back to the 1700s. Renowned ghost investigators Ed and Lorraine Warren once showed me a video Ed captured of the White Lady. He had his video camera set on a tripod at the gate of the cemetery at night, and from the right-hand side of the picture, a misty white form takes shape into the outline of a human (presumably a woman), then weaves between several headstones and into the clearing just before the gate. As "she" gets closer to the camera, some dark blobs seem to jump at her from near her feet before she dissipates into the ground. The entire video lasts maybe 5 or 6 seconds but is among the most compelling footage I've ever seen.

The Warrens' book, *Graveyard*, says the White Lady was a murder victim from the 1800s, and her body was dumped behind the Easton Baptist Church. The building is a picturesque white-steepled, old New England church that sits at the north end of the cemetery.

DeCaro and I walked through Union Cemetery as he spoke about his experiences when he had started regularly taking these photographs. He said, "At first my wife was a little nervous because, when I started to do this, the first night out, I'm getting orbs. The second night out I'm getting spooky mists, and then I start getting these faces. Almost every time out, I'm coming back with something. Three or four weeks into it, things started to happen around the house like doors opening, drawers opening, glasses moving when you go to reach for it, things like that. She started yelling, 'What are you doing down there?'" He can smile about it now, but this marked the beginning of DeCaro's deeper understanding of the spirit world. He would name his practice of spirit communication via the camera "spiritography."

Back at DeCaro's home, we went through some of his vast collection of images containing many different anomalies and spirit matter. He showed me photos of vortexes, with swirling mists and orbs around it. "I actually saw this happen, and then I took the picture," he said. We went through other apparition images; some looked remarkably human, others looked like some kind of monster—not like any animal I've ever seen. There were dozens and dozens of pictures, all containing something profound.

When DeCaro takes spirit photographs, he shoots digital and he does it alone. "To me, this is a very personal process," he said. "I approach this as a form of spirit communication, and as such, any successes and/or failures become a learning process for further advancement in that communication. Spirit photography is an aided type of mediumship—using the camera to communicate with spirits, or rather, using the camera to let spirits communicate with you. When, how, or why the spirits choose to appear or make contact is of their doing."

At Ghostvillage.com, I've published many dozens of spirit photos over the years. There's an online form where I ask people to try to remember as much of the who, what, when, where, and why details as possible. Certainly I understand that many anomalous photos are often taken by accident, so people may not remember the details, because they weren't trying to capture anything supernatural, but there are many common mistakes people can make.

For example, back in September, when I was in the Devil's Den battlefields in Gettysburg, there was a strange phenomenon happening in the fields, where an area reaching roughly 3 feet from the ground—up to the tops of the tall grass and weeds— was very cool, even though the night was warm,. There was a thin trail that led to a round clearing over a large rock about 15 feet into the fields. I walked in there with my camera and squatted down. The field was completely dark so there was no point in looking through my viewfinder. I held the camera at chest level and clicked the following picture.

I checked my LCD monitor immediately after taking the photograph and was stunned. I know there was no mist in front of me when I shot this picture. Photo by Jeff Belanger.

I showed the people with me what I had taken and received a few *ooohs* and *aahhs*, but something just didn't sit right with me.

I went back a few minutes later to the same spot and took another picture in the same fashion. This one had nothing in it. Then I took one more, but I exhaled a second before I clicked the picture. The following picture is what I got.

Similar results to the first picture, but I know I was exhaling. The camera caught the mist of my breath. Photo by Jeff Belanger.

Here are some tips to help you rule out natural explanations for photo anomalies:

- Carry a small notebook with you to jot a few notes down regarding the environment in which you took the photo.
- Note what kind of equipment you are using: what type of camera, what film speed (if applicable), what were the camera settings, etc.
- Make sure there are no camera straps or that you're not wearing any clothing or jewelry that could inadvertently pass in front of the camera lens.

- Note the time, date, and location.
- Note weather conditions. If you have a thermometer, all the better, but at the very least note if it's cool, damp, warm, dry, etc. Can you see your breath?
- Don't smoke during your photography session.
- If using film, store it in a cool, dry environment—such as your refrigerator—both before and after using it, and get it developed at a higher-end studio. You may pay a little extra, but it will limit the developing and printing errors that can occur.

These guidelines are designed to help you control your environment and experiment. If you are getting anomalous photos after going through the precautions, it certainly adds more credence to your images.

Another trend I've noticed, after having reviewed hundreds of purported spirit images, is people seeing faces and other human features in photographs. Sometimes these human-like figures are noticed within strange mists that appear in the photographs—those examples, I think, are among the most intriguing. But I've also noticed that people will have a picture of a cloud in the sky, or a photo of a line of trees and say, "See the face in that tree?"

After the September 11 attacks on the World Trade Center, there was a photo taken by the Associated Press that was passed all over the Internet and was even printed in many newspapers with the caption, "Is this the face of evil?" The way the black smoke is pouring out of the damaged, burning buildings in the picture does indeed resemble a giant, demonic face. But people tend to see faces everywhere. We're programmed that way. Like most people, I hardly ever forget a face. And think of the nature of faces—two eyes, a nose, a mouth, maybe some facial hair, maybe brown eyes, maybe blue, a few different skin tones. It's incredible that we can memorize many thousands of faces considering how very similar they all are.

I spoke to my sister, Susan Belanger, Ph.D., about this very topic. She happens to be a practicing behavioral psychologist, and I highly recommend that everyone have at least one in their family.

"What the hell are you working on now?" Dr. Belanger asked.

"Tell me about pattern recognition," I said. "Specifically, our ability to perceive faces."

This isn't the first time I've called on my sister for help with psychology. We've gotten to the point in our relationship where she answers my inquiries now with very few questions asked...which is nice.

"Have you heard of Rorschach testing?" she asked.

"You mean the series of inkblots on cards?"

"Right. That test has been in use for decades. Psychologists have been studying and trying to normalize responses to the test. Preadolescents and children who take the Rorschach tend to see less human representations and more animal representations. As you get older—adolescents and adults—you expect to have a certain amount of human representation in the responses. It might not be faces exactly, but faces are one thing that you might see."

The Rorschach test was developed by Hermann Rorschach (1884–1922) and introduced in 1921. It is comprised of a series of inkblots on cards that respondents are asked to give their first impression of. The actual shape of the Rorschach inkblots are a guarded secret in the psychology world, because if the images were widely distributed and seen by too many people, the test results would be skewed and meaningless.

"So an older Rorschach respondent is more likely to see human features in the cards?" I asked.

"There's absolutely an expectation that, if a normal adult sees 10 cards, he or she will give between 15 and 20 responses with a certain amount of human representation in those responses. Children are more likely to see animal patterns or other shapes."

"Would there be any difference in Rorschach tests and seeing shapes in the clouds?"

"No difference," she said. "Other than the fact that it's [Rorschach is] standardized, nothing. We have norms for the cards, we don't have norms for the clouds. But anybody could make a Rorschach test."

In other words, it seems that we're programmed to find and recognize faces in shapes and patterns everywhere we look.

Spirit Photography Samples

This orb photo was taken in Gettysburg, Pennsylvania, on September 25, 2004, at 9:20 p.m. Photo by Jeff Belanger.

I have rarely tried to take spirit photographs. On this occasion in Gettysburg, I was consciously trying. I took the previous picture at one of the monuments in the Wheat Fields section of the Gettysburg battlefields. I personally feel orbs are very inconclusive, but the photo shows what my camera captured. There are two orbs— one on the left and a smaller one on the right.

This picture of an energy streak was taken at Cochem Castle in Cochem, Germany, during a tour in October 2003. Photo by Denise Wendt.

Cochem Castle was built around 1000 C.E. and is located about 50 miles south of the city of Bonn, in the western part of Germany. Danielle Fisk and her mother, Denise Wendt, were touring the castle when an energy streak picture was taken. Fisk said, "My mother was here in Germany visiting me, and we went on a tour of the Castle. I have believed in spirits for a long time, but that was the first time I have ever seen a picture! We were following behind the main group, as we like to look closer at things. My mother was in the room behind me, and I was watching her and waiting for her to catch up. She took a picture and then called me over to look at the picture in the preview screen on the back of the digital camera. She thought she had messed up the camera somehow and wanted me to fix it. I told her it was a ghost—which she really didn't want to believe—and to take another picture. The second picture has nothing on it. She now has a stronger belief in spirits."

Fisk claims that neither she nor her mom saw or felt anything strange when the previous picture was taken with her Sony digital camera.

This anomaly was captured at Gunntown Cemetery in Naugatuck, Connecticut, on January 15, 2004. Photo by Kyle DeVack.

Cathy Johnson and her son, Kyle DeVack, are regular visitors to Gunntown Cemetery in Naugatuck, Connecticut. The cemetery was established in 1790 and is regarded locally as both historic and haunted. "There's one story of the spirit of a horse that travels through the yard and through the back field there," Johnson said. "Another story is that you can hear and see black dogs running around—they're shadowy figures, not actual dogs. You hear children laughing and playing—I've heard that myself."

Gunntown is a very small cemetery that contains more than 460 graves—they're tightly packed, to say the least. Johnson claims she gets an uneasy feeling whenever she and her son visit the graveyard. She describes it as a feeling as though thousands of bugs are crawling all over you, so she stays on the other side of the wall just outside the grounds and takes pictures. On a typical night, they will shoot three or four rolls of film and also bring a digital camera.

The previous mist photo was taken by Kyle. "He said he heard something like a whisper, or rustling, or maybe a tree branch moving behind him," Johnson said. "He turned around and there it was. He didn't see it face-to-face—he just took a picture. And that's how it came out."

This picture of Simone Mayberry, of Mt. Eliza, Victoria, in Australia, was taken by her friend in 1992. When she saw the print, she was taken by the vortex in the image. Photo courtesy of Simone Mayberry.

The preceding picture was taken at Morning Star Estate, built by Francis A. Gillet, of London, in 1853. According to Simone Mayberry, the picture was taken with an old 110mm Kodak Instamatic camera that had no strap. I asked her if she had intended to try and take a spirit photo. She said, "No. I was doing an online search for webcams and found all of these wonderful links to ghost cams and ghost groups. And over time I realized that I myself may have some photos with paranormal activity in them."

This picture was taken using an infrared setting, during a ceremonial circle in a cemetery in Flat Rock, Michigan, in the summer of 2002. Photo by Dennis Lytle.

Dennis Lytle was visiting a cemetery with some people who are psychically sensitive. This venture was not about simply capturing a spirit on camera for Lytle; for him it was also a spiritual venture. "The cemetery is old, neglected, and has been desecrated," he said of the location. "On a previous trip, we had successfully photographed several orbs and spirit manifestations. I set up a return trip there specifically to try to help the one I had photographed return home."

According to Lytle, the previous image was taken with his Sony digital camcorder (model TRV-340-NTSC) using an 8 LED infrared emitter. His decision to try infrared came after a discussion with a friend of his who claimed that his cat seemed to react to something unseen. Lytle said, "The main difference between some animals' eyes and a human eye is the ability to perceive light better, even into the near-infrared area of the spectrum. So following up on my suggestion to try filming the area in infrared, he borrowed a Sony with nightshot. The following day he showed me a moving orb he recorded when his cat freaked out in the bedroom. I realized that something unseen had just been revealed by infrared technology. I bought my own Sony camcorder and started my investigations of the paranormal."

I asked Lytle what he thought the infrared revealed. He explained how one of the psychically sensitive people there had a vision of a Manitou—a Native American spirit energy. "The sensitive said the Manitou had his arms outstretched and had white light springing out of his chest," Lytle said. "She said Indians were running toward us and jumping into the light. I was skeptical, to say the least. Even though I felt strange, deep chills passing through my body—now I realize this was the result of spirits passing through me—I passed it all off as being imagination. Imagine my astonishment when reviewing the videotape to see the head of an Indian warrior actually within the circle! The height was right for men of that period, the head showed a Mohawk haircut, and when enhanced for contrast/brightness, it was obviously an Indian warrior. My skepticism took a direct hit that day."

This photo was taken during an investigation at the Governor Sprague Mansion in Cranston, Rhode Island, in March 2003. Photo courtesy of the Rhode Island Paranormal Research Group.

The Rhode Island Paranormal Research Group (TRIPRG) visits the haunted Governor Sprague mansion every year to conduct an ongoing investigation. I contacted Andrew Laird, the group's founder and director, about the preceding photo, shot there by his group. "It was taken by our Audio-Visual Engineer," Laird said. "He often used what we refer to as an ordinary 35mm Kodak 'checkout line' disposable camera—with surprisingly good success."

"What made him take this picture at this moment?" I asked. "Was it random?"

"That particular evening, he had decided to set up his recording equipment in the ballroom, an area of the mansion that is known for its paranormal activity," Laird said. "It was during an attempt to record EVP when he observed both a noticeable, sudden dip in the temperature and an unexplainable static coming through his headphones. Taking a quick meter reading, he found the area to be 'hot' but just within the immediate area of his work station. That was when he decided to snap the picture."

Spirit photographic evidence certainly becomes more weighty when combined with other controlled experiments such as a sudden change in temperature and a spike in electromagnetic activity. Paranormal investigative groups such as TRIPRG are certainly adding credibility to this phenomena.

Film cameras can and do see faster than the human eye is able, and digital cameras can not only see faster, but in a slightly broader spectrum than our own eyes. This simple fact certainly adds to the intrigue of spirit photography. Spirit photography offers some of the most profound supernatural evidence there is—especially for the photographer. It's an image that can be shown to others and something that can beg us to wonder if we just caught a glimpse of the spirit world or if the spirit world has physically affected our photography equipment to leave us a sign.

"Pluralitas non est ponenda sine necessitate"—plurality should not be posited without necessity. This is Occam's razor, named for medieval philosopher and Franciscan monk William of Ockham (1285–1349). More plainly put, the simplest explanation is usually the correct one. When reviewing potential spirit photographs, I apply Occam's razor first. Once I've exhausted all of the simple explanations, I have my own spiritual experience in regard to the image. Those are my own "Wow!" moments—the experiences that force me to ask more questions of myself and of the world around me.

"I am inclined to believe that our personality hereafter will be able to affect matter.
If this reasoning be correct, then, if we can evolve an instrument so delicate as to be affected, or moved, or manipulated—whichever term you want to use—by our personality as it survives in the next life, such an instrument, when made available, ought to record something."

Thomas Edison's Lost Spirit Communication Apparatus

When Thomas Alva Edison was a little boy, he wanted to figure out how the telegraph worked—but not just how it worked, *why* it worked. In 1921, Edison wrote that the best explanation he ever got was from an old Scotsman who was a telegraph line repairman. The Scotsman said that if you had a dog that was long enough to reach from Edinburgh to London, like a dachshund, and you pulled his tail in Edinburgh, the dog would bark in London. "I could understand that," Edison wrote. "But it was hard to get at what it was that went through the dog or over the wire." He would spend his entire life trying to figure out mysteries such as these.

Thomas Edison's vision and incredible intellect led to inventions such as the lightbulb, phonograph, film projector, and storage battery, among many others; he had more than 1,000 patents to his name and is one of the founders of the General Electric company. This self-taught man of science worked tirelessly in the pursuit of making our lives better through devices that lit our way, improved our mobility, and facilitated communication. By the time Edison died on October 18, 1931, his inventions and enhancements to existing inventions, such as motors, electric railways, telephones, dynamos, and more, helped build industries worth many billions of dollars.

Thomas Edison. Photo courtesy of the Library of Congress.

What would this logical and successful man of science be doing trying to communicate with the spirit world? Or experimenting with the occult for that matter? Many Edison historians would prefer that the great inventor's dabbling in the supernatural was a skeleton that stayed in his closet. Some claim Edison was swindled by Spiritualists late in his life when he may have been growing senile, and that it explains some of his comments about spirit communication. But in looking closer, it seems Edison always had an affinity for the supernatural. This was a man who thrived on solving problems, and the question of a personality surviving death would be the greatest challenge ever solved, if he could do it.

Born in Milan, Ohio, on February 11, 1847, Edison lost most of his hearing during childhood. By his teens, he was legally deaf. His poor hearing may account for the fact that he was never a good student in school, and communicating was always a challenge because of it. In 1863, he began working as a telegraph operator. The concept of long-distance communication intrigued him. The telegraph was less than 20 years old at the time Edison took the telegraph operator job; it was an industry still in its infancy. Electronic communication began on May 24, 1844, when Samuel F.B. Morse's message transferred from Washington to Baltimore through code.

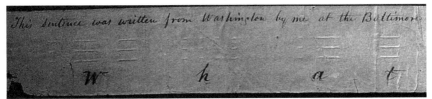

This close-up view shows the first word of Samuel Morse's written note, "What Hath God Wrought," sent electronically from Washington to Baltimore by the first telegraph operator. Photo courtesy of the Library of Congress.

With the telegraph, scientists discovered how to transfer thoughts and words into energy and then send them along a wire so a person on the receiving end, many miles away, could understand the message. As with any breakthrough, other scientists began to ask more questions and wonder how far the concept could be pushed. If beeps or clicks could be sent many miles through a wire, could a voice? How about a picture? The leap to spirit communication really wasn't that far, considering the miracle unfolding through the wires in the mid-19th century.

To understand more about Thomas Edison, his work, and his interest in the supernatural, I spoke with Laurence J. Russell, curator for the Edison Birthplace Museum (*www.tomedison.org*) in Milan, Ohio. The Birthplace Museum was opened by Edison's widow, Mina Miller Edison, and his second daughter, Madeline Sloane, in 1947. Russell has worked at the museum since 1965 and had the opportunity to work for Mrs. Sloane for 10 years.

Being around the museum for so long, Russell is full of anecdotes about Thomas Edison that have been passed on to him first- and secondhand from the museum's visitors and from Mrs. Sloane herself. Russell recounted one story Mrs. Sloane told him about a time Edison brought the children outside during a thunderstorm, pointed skyward, and said, "There's a great engineer up there."

Edison's interest in the supernatural may have begun with his study of the work of German chemist Baron Karl von Reichenbach (1788–1869). In the 1850s, Reichenbach claimed he discovered a mysterious force that could explain supernatural phenomena—he named this force "Od," after the Norse god Odin. The force would be referred to as "Odyle" or "Odic" by Reichenback's contemporaries.

Od, Reichenbach theorized, is the natural power created by physical and/or energetic forces such as magnets, heat, light, or chemicals to produce the phenomena of *mesmerism*—or hypnotic magnetism—the result being visions or special powers such as telepathy or telekinesis. Basically, this German scientist was acknowledging that the supernatural is a real force in the world, and because the concept didn't fit in with the science of the time (and it still doesn't today), Reichenbach used the theory of Odyle force to clean up the scientific inconsistencies. Od was a way to try to give supernatural phenomena validity and make it more palatable to the scientific community. His theories on this "new force" were not accepted by most scientists.

Edison, though, thought the idea of this mysterious energy was at least plausible—and he wasn't the only scientist to explore the idea. Chemist Sir William Crookes (1832–1919) also began to explore the claims of psychics and spiritualists, and his position on the subject was similar to Edison's. Crookes wrote, "I consider it the duty of scientific men who have learnt exact modes of working to examine phenomena which attract the attention of the public, in order to confirm their genuineness or to explain, if possible, the delusions of the dishonest and to expose the tricks of deceivers."

Crookes developed the "Crookes Tube"—an early vacuum tube that would help further the concept of electric lighting. He also discovered the element thallium and was a respected scientist his entire life. In his explorations of Spiritualism, he found more questions than answers. There is even a photograph I've seen of Sir William Crookes with the alleged "spirit image" of his deceased wife, Lady Crookes.

Crookes and Edison corresponded with each other. There are claims that Crookes showed some spirit photographs to Edison—something that further fueled Edison's fire to find a way to discover the force behind the supernatural.

In Paul Israel's book, *Edison: A Life of Invention*, the author discusses an experiment Edison conducted in November of 1875. Edison was working on an acoustic telegraph in Western Union's laboratory that could send multiple telegraph messages through the same wire simultaneously—a critical enhancement needed if the telegraph was going to enjoy more widespread use and lower operating costs.

In the experiment, he used a vibrator magnet—a device that produced incredibly rapid, continuous vibrations—as an automatic circuit breaker. The electromagnet was charged by a battery that attracted a metal lever on a pivot. The lever was parallel to the magnet cores and sat on a contact point. When the magnet was turned on, it lifted the lever off of the contact point, which then broke the circuit, turning the magnet off and allowing the lever to drop back down, completing the circuit again and continuing the cycle. During the tests, Edison and his staff noticed a spark passing between the magnet cores and the metal lever. At first they thought the sparks were similar to those they observed in stock ticker machines—sparks that occurred when some tiny iron filings came between the armature and the core and between the core and the electric pen that wrote the stock results on the ticker tape. The stock ticker spark was caused by the process of induction; the iron filings would get charged by the power source and momentarily ground as they bounced around. But this spark was different. Edison and his staff found they could get a spark by touching the vibrator with a piece of iron. When they used a larger piece of iron, the spark became larger. The researchers found they could make the spark jump from the machine to any point in the room where the iron bar was placed. This energy spark didn't register on their galvanometer—a device used to detect, measure, and determine the direction of electric currents—meaning the charge had no polarity. Edison concluded in his notes that the "cause of the spark is a true unknown force."

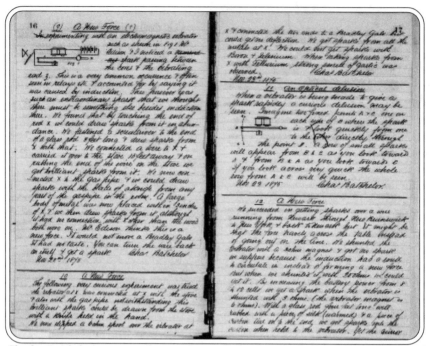

Charles Batchelor's notes on the experiments Edison's team conducted when they found the new force.

Edison began referring to this new force as "etheric force." He felt etheric force could be used to send telegraph messages along railroad tracks or through uninsulated wires. Certain that he made a genuine breakthrough, Edison called a press conference on November 29, 1875.

The December 2nd *New York Herald* wrote the following attributed to Edison:

> Under certain conditions heat energy can be transmitted into electric energy, and that again, under certain conditions, into magnetic energy, this back again into electric energy, all forms of energy being interchangeable with each other. It follows that if electric energy under certain conditions is transformed into that of magnetism under other conditions it might be transformed into an entirely unknown force, subject to laws different from

those of heat, light, electricity or magnetism.
There is every reason to suppose that etheric
energy is this new form.

Other newspapers reported that Edison believed
Reichenbach's odic force was indeed his etheric force. By April
of the following year, just five months later, researchers determined that Edison's etheric force was actually the result of
opposite induced currents—not some new force. Etheric force
was dismissed from the scientific community.

The point is, as Paul Israel notes in his book, Edison was so
quick to claim this discovery because he was actively looking for
this new force. This wasn't the end of Edison's foray into the
supernatural, however—only the beginning.

Henry Olcott, a cofounder of the American Theosophical
Society, said in his book *Old Diary Leaves: The True Story of
the Theosophical Society* that Edison connected various kinds of
conductors—fluid-filled tubes and wires of different thickness
and metals—to a pendulum. He would then place the other end
of the conductor against his forehead and try to move the
pendulum with his mind. He was testing whether his thought
patterns (which are electrical impulses, after all) could travel
along the wires or tubes and force some movement.

Edison's interest in these supernatural forces ran deeper than
just his own curiosity in understanding the ethereal. He was a
capitalist by nature and saw many practical applications for this
kind of ability. Could occult forces drive communication across
great distances by using a new source of power? And if we could
control that new force, could we then communicate with those
who have passed on?

In a January 1911 interview in *The Columbian Magazine*,
Edison discussed his testing of the seemingly superhuman
powers of Professor Bert Reese of New York City. In the interview
Edison said:

He plainly showed a certain power which cannot
be laughed to scorn, cannot be at present satisfac-
torily explained away. A century ago, the man
would have been looked upon as a wizard. In the

early days of Massachusetts, a woman with such powers as his would certainly have been burned for witchcraft, yet Reese, though unexplainable at present, is a mere prodigy. He makes startling claims for his ability and some of these he demonstrates. We all saw him read words which had been written in rooms distant from the one in which he had remained, and read them when the paper upon which they had been written remained folded and refolded. He claims other powers and may have them, for all we can say positively to the contrary. He is a prodigy, and, as a prodigy, is wonderful.

Evidence of Edison's interest in spiritual matters is found everywhere the man left his mark. Laurence Russell said. "Years ago, I went to Glenmont—his mansion in West Orange [New Jersey]," Russell said. "I was talking to Thelda Coakley who was the curator there. She had worked for Edison. We got to talking about this [Edison's spiritual interests] and she said, 'Well you know there are Spiritualist books in the library.' And she said, 'I always thought that he got them when he bought the house—from the man who built the house—but maybe not.'"

Edison's daughter, Madeline Sloane, claimed her father was a deist—meaning he believed there was a supreme creator who came in long ago, created the earth and everything in it, then walked away to let it run itself. He believed when we die, our bodies simply rot away. But there's a "but...."

"He had this idea that everything was made up of little particles called 'swarms of life units,'" Russell said. "And when people died, they went on and became something else."

In 1948, Philosophical Library published a book called *The Diary and Sundry Observations of Thomas Alva Edison*, a collection of Edison's personal journal entries, essays, and interviews. The book covers his thoughts on contacting the dead and the afterlife extensively. When it was published, the work was so controversial that some members of Edison's family, as well as some of his surviving associates, took enough action against the publisher to force them to put out a revised edition of the book that is 66 pages shorter, with any mention of the supernatural removed. The revised edition, however, makes no mention of being "revised"—the copyright pages of both books imply that they are first editions. In the *original* first edition of the book, Edison said of the subject of the afterlife:

> The thing which first struck me was the absurdity of expecting "spirits" to waste their time operating such cumbrous, unscientific media as tables, chairs, and the Ouija board with its letters. My convinced belief is merely that if ever the question of life after death, or psychic phenomena generally, is to be solved, it will have to be put on a scientific basis, as chemistry is put, and withdrawn from the hands of charlatan and the "medium."

The "swarms of life units" Mr. Russell mentioned are described in detail in the original version of the book, in Edison's essay titled "Life After Death," which was written in 1922. He believed each of us—every living thing, for that matter—is made up of billions of units of life. These units are smaller than cells, so microscopically small that he believed they could even pass through glass. These life units work in harmony (and sometimes discord) within large groups to control what kind of person you are, your level of intelligence, creativity, moral standing, and so on. He postulated that these units have memory and record everything they see. If you burn your finger, for instance, the skin will grow back with the same fingerprint as before because of the memory of these life units. And the units, like matter, cannot be destroyed. When they're finished with their job (that is, when our bodies die), the life units dissipate and carry our memories with them. Edison thought that certain life units were the controllers of others and they resided in the part of the brain known as the *Broca*, where he believed our personalities are housed. Edison wrote:

> The point is whether these directing entities remain together after the death of the body in which they have been residing, or whether they go about the universe after breaking up. If they break up

and no longer remain as an ensemble, then it looks to me that our personality does not survive death; that is, we do not survive death as individuals.

If they do break up and do not remain together after the death of the body, then that would mean that the eternal life which so many of us earnestly desire would not be the eternal life and persistence of the individual, as individual, but would be an impersonal eternal life—for, whatever happens to the life units, or whatever forms they may assume, it is at least assured that they themselves live forever.

It was around 1920 that Edison really began to experiment with the concept of spirit communication—though he would never have called it "spirit communication." He would have said he was trying to build a device to detect the life units that contained a deceased person's personality and memory and allow those life units to cause intelligent responses to his apparatus. This may sound like semantics to some—okay, even to me—but Edison was a deist and didn't believe in a soul or spirit in the traditional religious sense.

In a 1920 essay titled "Spiritualism," Edison wrote:

I am proceeding on the theory that in the very nature of things, the degree of material or physical power possessed by those in the next life must be extremely slight; and that, therefore, any instrument designed to be used to communicate with us must be super-delicate—as fine and responsive as human ingenuity can make it. For my part, I am inclined to believe that our personality hereafter will be able to affect matter. If this reasoning be correct, then, if we can evolve an instrument so delicate as to be affected, or moved, or manipulated—whichever term you want to use—by our personality as it survives in the next life, such an instrument, when made available, ought to record something.

Today there are many rumors about a machine he was trying to build during the last decade of his life—a machine that could communicate with the dead. Many Edison historians scoff at the notion. But Edison was in fact working on such a device. Also included in the original printing of *The Diary and Sundry Observations of Thomas Alva Edison*, in an essay called "Spirit Communication," written in 1920, Edison wrote:

> Now what I propose to do is furnish psychic investigators with an apparatus which will give a scientific aspect to their work. This apparatus, let me explain, is in the nature of a valve, so to speak. That is to say, the slightest conceivable effort is made to exert many times its initial power for indicative purposes. It is similar to a modern power house, where man, with his relatively puny one-eighth horse-power, turns a valve which starts a 50,000-horse-power steam turbine. My apparatus is along those lines, in that the slightest effort which it intercepts will be magnified many times so as to give us whatever form of record we desire for the purpose of investigation. Beyond that I don't care to say anything further regarding its nature. I have been working out the details for some time; indeed, a collaborator in this work died only the other day. In that he knew exactly what I am after in this work, I believe he ought to be the first to use it if he is able to do so. Of course, don't forget that I am making no claims for the survival of personality; I am not promising communication with those who have passed out of this life. I merely state that I am giving the psychic investigators an apparatus which may help them in their work, just as optical experts have given the microscope to the medical world. And if this apparatus fails to reveal anything of exceptional interest, I am afraid that I shall have lost all faith in the survival of personality as we know it in this existence.

In another 1920 essay on Spiritualism, Edison wrote, "I have been at work for some time building an apparatus to see if it is possible for personalities which have left this earth to communicate with us...and I hope to be able to finish it before very many months pass."

Mentioning his apparatus again in a 1922 essay, Edison wrote, "...that does not mean that I believe the survival of personality had been proved—as yet. Perhaps it may be one day. Perhaps some apparatus upon the lines of my 'valve' may prove it, but that day is not yet...."

Edison spent years working on his "valve" apparatus. His long history of successful inventions and products are proof that he was no fool and not someone who was prone to chase an idea for multiple years if he didn't believe he could make some profound discovery.

For the rest of his days, Edison continued to invent, study, and try to figure out how things worked. On October 14, 1931, the work ended when Thomas Edison slipped into a coma. Shortly before he died on October 18, he woke from his coma and whispered to his wife, Mina, who had been keeping a vigil at his bedside, "It is very beautiful over there...."

No prototype, parts, or plans for Edison's spirit communication apparatus have ever been found. The only evidence of the machine today are his multiple references to it in his interviews and essays of the time. But the accounts of his spirit communication apparatus didn't end with his death.

According to Richard Winer and Nancy Osborn's 1979 book, *Haunted Houses*, in 1941, two of Thomas Edison's associates allegedly made contact with him during a séance in New York. In the séance, he claimed the plans and schematics for his apparatus were with three assistants. Edison said his valve was built, but didn't work. But the story continues. Reportedly in a second séance, Edison made some suggestions on alterations to the apparatus that would make it work. J. Gilbert Wright was present at the séance and claimed to make Edison's changes. Wright reportedly worked on the apparatus until his death in 1959. There's been no trace of Edison's "valve" since.

When Edison said the question of life after death or psychic phenomena will be solved by science and not the "medium," I don't think he realized that the very nature of scientific inquiry would need to change to be able to answer these questions. Edison had a hypothesis: that we are all made up of tiny swarms of life particles that never die. And he believed if he could simply make a machine sensitive enough, he could prove it. But his logic wasn't equipped to answer the question, though he did try. He tested, he sought evidence, and he explored the topic to the very best of his ability.

As a person who needs things proved to him, I can certainly appreciate a scientific approach to spiritual questions. But science during Edison's time and even today doesn't have the capacity to answer these questions. Science's accepted rules for logic and proof don't leave any room for personal interpretations. For example, if I tell you that Peanut M&M's are my favorite candy and I could eat them every day, would you have any reason to not believe me? I can tell you it's true. I know it for a fact. However, can science prove it to be true? Or untrue for that matter? Empirically, my love of Peanut M&Ms can't be measured and tested in a lab. We simply lack a way to ask the right questions.

Science and spirituality have a long way to go before they begin to mix, but it's critical that both sides continue to ask questions. A spirit-detecting apparatus is not listed among Edison's many noteworthy inventions, but his ideas and experiments in the subject make him a true forefather for Instrumental Transcommunication (ITC)—a concept that involves using electrical equipment to facilitate communication with spirits—something explored in more detail in coming chapters. If Edison had only lived another decade or so, maybe he would have stumbled upon the right questions regarding the afterlife; maybe today, next to our telephones in the kitchen would be a second device used for speaking with those who have already passed on. We'll never know. That day may still be coming, though. Edison might just be the first person I try to call.

"I was the one who played back that recording; in those 30 seconds at the end, there's this woman's voice and she said, 'I miss you, Lisa.' And I just about dropped my jaw. I didn't say anything, then I said, 'Hey, Tom, listen to this.' He said, 'My gosh, that's your mother.'"

# 5 Electronic Voice Phenomena

Did you hear that? Seriously, did you? Whispers, phantom voices, inner voices...we can always second-guess ourselves, but when these sounds are caught on tape, the second-guessing stops.

Electronic Voice Phenomenon, or EVP, is the term for unexpected, oftentimes unexplainable, disembodied voices captured via audio recording media. EVP is a subset of a larger field of study called Instrumental Transcommunication, or ITC, something we'll cover more in-depth in the next chapter.

For many, EVP offers a sound bite from the supernatural. Others have evolved the practice into a two-way conversation with the other side. EVP is being used by ghost hunters as potential evidence of a haunting. Some are using the practice as part of grief counseling, and others take that idea a step further to the point of continuing their relationship with a departed loved one who has died. The equipment required is nothing more than an audio recorder—and not necessarily even an expensive one. People are getting results with the most inexpensive equipment. But are the results truly voices from beyond the grave or some recording anomaly that has yet to be explained? Though some voices are very clear, others require some imagination. Is our brain simply looking for speech patterns in random noise, just as we seek human features in seemingly random images?

To grasp EVP, you'll have to lend me your ear—because that's ultimately the road any sound has to travel for us to interpret it. I spoke with Dr. Craig W. Johnson, Au.D., an audiologist with Audiology Associates, Inc. and president of the Academy of Dispensing Audiologists. He spoke to me from his office in Baltimore, Maryland.

We started with the very nature of sound. Sound travels in waves of vibrations. The quantity of these vibrations, or cycles per second, is called the frequency and is measured in hertz. One cycle per second is equal to one hertz. For a normal, healthy young person, the hearing range is about 60 to 20,000 hertz. Though, as Grandpa will tell you, hearing gets worse with age. Infrasound are those frequencies below the human range and ultrasound are those above human range. Many animals use ultrasound to communicate or navigate; a bat, for example, will detect frequencies up to 100,000 hertz.

Sounds are everywhere around us, traveling through the air, water, ground, and many other substances. "How does sound get into our brains?" I asked.

"Sound is a vibratory motion," Dr. Johnson said. "As the sound goes down the ear canal, it vibrates the ear drum first, which then, in turn, vibrates just as if you were talking into a snare drum. That vibration is sent through the tiniest bones in the body, called the *ossicles*—they are three little middle ear bones that are articulated in a way to help amplify the sound. Those vibrations are then sent into the inner ear where the first-order neurons are housed."

Dr. Johnson explained how these vibrations set ripples in motion through fluid in the inner ear, which then flows over many tiny hair cells that bend back and forth. These cells bend only two ways—on or off; there is no in-between.

"When the hair cells bend, they give off an electrical spark," Johnson said. "That signal then gets encoded in the auditory central nervous system, and then it's transmitted up to the brain."

"And in the brain we understand the sound?" I asked.

"Right," he said. "There are about eight different way stations on the path up to the brain from the inner ear. We call these way stations *synapses*—they control sound and serve as a gate. Once sound is perceived, there are two different things going on. There's hearing in terms of 'Can that person hear that signal?' And then there's a whole other thing going on which is perception—how is it perceived? And then you get into interpretation, understanding, comprehension, and eventually deal with all kinds of more complicated issues once that signal goes up to your noodle."

Dr. Johnson explained how there are two other types of nerves that also come into play in regard to our hearing. One is the *afferent* set of nerves, which are responsible for sending signals from the outside world up to the brain; the other is the *efferent* set of nerves, which moderate input, supressing sounds in noisy environments and augmenting sounds in quiet environments.

"If you've ever had the experience of walking into the woods, you notice that after about 15 or 20 seconds or so you can suddenly hear every little twig and every little leaf, and you feel like you have heightened sensitivity," Dr. Johnson said. "We never really thought too much about that until we understood how the efferent system works. The efferent system in the auditory system is responsible for two things. First off, it's responsible for enhancing very soft sounds. So if you're sitting around the house and there's no one there and you're turning pages of a book, all of a sudden the sound of the turning pages becomes very enhanced—it's the same kind of experience you have in the woods. What the efferent system does is actually enhance the hair cell performance. The little hair cells actually protrude so they can reach the membrane in the inner ear a little sooner and increase amplitude. Conversely, if you go into a noisy place, such as a restaurant or a bar, these hair cells retract—they actually pull down and shrink inside."

This is important because otherwise you could be distracted by everything in an environment with a lot going on. The efferent nerves help you tune out what isn't important.

In regards to speech, we're generally concerned with the 500 to 3,000 hertz range, though the frequencies above 3,000 also play a factor. Telephones typically cover 500 to 3,000 hertz because manufacturers can keep the costs down by not putting in more expensive equipment than is necessary.

We don't always recognize voices over the phone if we've only spoken with the person once or twice, though if that person was standing close to us—but hidden from our sight—we may recognize his voice because of the specifics in the higher frequencies within his speech. This is important to keep in mind with regard to recording sounds. The more frequencies within a recording, the more likely our brains are to process the sounds better.

Humans have a natural proclivity for recognizing speech. We look for recognizable patterns in every sound we hear. Wind blowing through trees is processed in one part of the brain because we may not need to know anything more about this ambient sound (assuming the wind isn't so strong as to blow trees down on us). But other sounds that have distinct patterns are important for our brains to process more carefully. We look for words in every sound because we are constantly looking for important information—warnings of danger, the sounds of loved ones who may be close by, questions that may be asked of us, or even announcements as to how long our flights will be delayed. We thrive on information and communication and depend on sounds in the form of speech to give us an edge in our daily lives and on a broader evolutionary scale.

Hearing another's voice also tells us we aren't alone. The day science made the breakthrough that allowed us to record our voices and play them back was a day modern civilization took a giant step forward.

"Mary had a little lamb whose fleece was white as snow, and everywhere that Mary went, the lamb was sure to go" were the first human words ever recorded onto a device called a phonograph—the first audio recorder that could also play the sound back. The date was December 4, 1877, and the man's voice was Thomas Alva Edison, who was working on the telegraph and telephone and who wanted to come up with a way to record messages to be played back later. Edison said of his invention, "This tongueless, toothless instrument, without larynx or pharynx, mimics your tones, speaks with your voice, utters your words and centuries after you have crumbled into dust, may repeat every idle thought, every fond fancy, every vain word that you choose to whisper against the thin, iron diaphragm."

Thomas Alva Edison with his phonograph, circa 1878–1880. Photo courtesy of the Library of Congress.

Edison's remarks about offering a way for people to speak—long after they're dead and turned to dust—were eerily foreboding. Some may even call his statement a premonition.

Edison's invention was ground-breaking, but it didn't have practical use for the masses. Though recording one's voice was certainly a neat trick, the device, in its earliest days, was prohibited by cost from gaining a place in every American home. In the coming decade, new inventions such as the Gramophone enabled people to play prerecorded wax cylinders of music in their homes. The Gramophone couldn't record, but it could play music—allowing those who could afford the device the ability to have symphonies and big bands perform on demand.

Recording phonographs did become available in the final years of the 1800s and worked much the same as Edison's first recorder. The user spoke into the mouth of a horn that funneled the sound through a needle that etched the voice onto a recording cylinder.

The first mention of disembodied voices caught in a recording came in 1901 when American ethnologist Waldemar Bogoras took his recording equipment to Spain to witness a Tchouktchi tribal spirit conjuring ritual. Bogoras set up his recorder in a room that was then darkened, and only he and the village shaman were in the room during the recording. The shaman steadily beat a drum to put himself into a trance, and as the ceremony proceeded, Bogoras claimed he heard voices speaking English and Russian coming from various parts of the room. When he played his recording back, he heard the steady volume of the drum—proving the shaman never left the spot he was in—as well as the spirit voices. It took a few more decades for recording equipment to become more practical and portable, and to produce a higher quality of recordings.

In the 1920s, radio spread to the masses and recording devices soon followed. The microphone technology needed for the broadcasts, combined with demand for portable recording devices so reporters could cover events such as meetings, sports, and other civic goings-on, drove the technology forward.

It was 1936 when someone used recording equipment with the intent of making spirit contact. Attila von Szalay was a psychic who claimed to hear spirit voices around him constantly. He used an old record cutter to try and capture these voices, but he was largely unsuccessful. Most of the credit for "discovering" EVP goes to Friedrich Jürgenson—a Swedish painter, musician, and singer. In 1957, he bought his first tape recorder to record his singing. During his early recording sessions, Jürgenson noticed he was getting strange fade-ins and fade-outs on the tapes. He also claimed to be receiving visions and messages from beyond. He believed his artistic proclivity made him more sensitive to these kind of messages. By tuning in, his psychic senses were being rapidly developed.

Jürgenson's breakthrough happened June 12, 1959, around 4 p.m. He and his wife, Monica, had gone to their country house outside of Stockholm for the weekend. Jürgenson brought his tape recorder outside to try and capture the songs of the wild birds.

When he played the tape back, he heard a noise he described as a "roaring, hissing static sound" that almost drowned out the chirping of the birds in the background. In Jürgenson's book, *Sprechfunk mit Verstorbenen* (*Voice Transmissions with the Deceased*), Jürgenson wrote:

> My first thought was that one of the tubes was damaged during the trip. Nevertheless, I turned the recorder on again and let the tape run. My second recording was just like before: I was hearing this strange hissing and the distant bird chirping. Then all of a sudden there sounded a trumpet solo as if to announce something. I listened with continued surprise as suddenly a male voice began to speak in Norwegian. Though it was very quiet, I could clearly understand the words. The man was talking about 'bird songs at night,' and I heard a number of chattering, whistling and splashing sounds, and among them what seemed to be the chirping of a sparrow.
>
> Suddenly the bird choir fell silent and with that so did the hissing sound. In the next instant the twittering of a finch was audible and in the distance you could hear a titmouse—the tape recorder was working perfectly again.

Did the tape recorder pick up a radio broadcast? That's what Jürgenson believed at first. But there was no radio receiver with him or anywhere near his isolated location. He did speculate on the timing and content of the message: "Wasn't it remarkable, that I of all people who was searching for bird sounds should receive sounds of Norwegian night birds exactly in that moment when I turned on the tape recorder? Was there an invisible intelligence that with such a remarkable way was trying to get my attention? Very puzzling!"

Friedrich Jürgenson is considered the father of EVP, and it was this event on that June day in 1959 that launched his research into the phenomenon. Jürgenson went on to record thousands of EVPs up until his death in 1987.

The American Association of Electronic Voice Phenomena, or AA-EVP (*www.aaevp.com*), was founded in 1982 by Sarah Estep. Their newsletter states their mission: "To provide objective evidence that we survive death in an individual conscious state." I spoke with Tom and Lisa Butler, a husband-and-wife team who have been involved in the organization since 1989, but took over leadership in May 2000. I spoke with the Butlers from their home in Reno, Nevada. Tom has a B.S. degree in Electronics Engineering and Lisa has a B.A. in Psychology. A pretty good pair for this, don't you think?

The Butlers first garnered interest in EVP when Lisa read Sarah Estep's book, *Voices of Eternity*. At the time, the Butlers were both high-level management workers in a big corporation. "I look back now and say, 'Gosh how could you believe that?'" Lisa said. "But I read the book and somehow it hit me in the gut that it was possible. After I read the book, it actually took me about a year to decide to try experimenting."

Lisa explained how her dad was an electrical engineer who had passed away a few years prior to her experiment. "It seemed logical that, gee, an engineer—this [EVP] might be something that he would try to communicate through," Lisa said. "Interestingly enough, he never did. My mother did, and she was the last person in the world that I would have expected. We were doing a big presentation in Canada, and before we do a presentation, we'll often do a recording and try and ask some questions that the group might be interested in," Lisa said. She had genuine nostalgia in her voice recalling this event. "So we did a recording, and at the end of recording, we've learned to say, 'We're going to turn this off now—you've got 30 seconds if there is anything you want to say.'

"We did that, and I was the one who played back that recording; in those 30 seconds at the end, there's this woman's voice and she said, 'I miss you, Lisa.' And I just about dropped my jaw. I didn't say anything, then I said, 'Hey, Tom, listen to this.' He said, 'My gosh, that's your mother.'"

I have an old General Electric handheld recorder that takes full-sized cassette tapes and that I've been using for years when

I do interviews. This machine today would probably cost less than $20. It's got a great built-in microphone for capturing my voice and the people I interview. While transposing interviews and writing articles, I've listened to hundreds of hours of tape that the machine recorded. I've never intentionally tried to record EVP with it, but sometimes there are strange sounds and noises that I've heard come off of my tapes. Because my recording sessions were for another purpose, any anomalous sounds I captured are pretty inconclusive. Although, according to the Butlers, my tape recorder may not be the best equipment for capturing EVP.

"In the early days with the reel-to-reel [recording equipment], people were getting EVP," Lisa Butler said. "We went from reel-to-reel to cassette decks and the EVP decreased. And now with the IC recorders, more people are getting EVP again."

"Are those digital recorders?" I asked.

"Right, that's digital," Tom Butler said. "The generic term we've been using for them is IC, or Integrated Circuit recorders. It's all solid state."

Tom explained how the old reel-to-reel recorders utilized vacuum tubes. Cassettes mainly utilize bipolar transistors, and with them, the amount and quality of EVP recordings dropped. He explained how the IC recorders' transistors behave more like the old vacuum tubes. So what does this mean?

"What we're seeing are hints that say that they [the otherworld entities] are actually telekinetically putting the information into the junction for the transistors or the plasma of the vacuum tube. We think that this is the concept of *stochastic resonance*."

"Stochastic resonance" took some research on my part. Essentially it means that a weak signal—in our case, a spirit voice—can be amplified by combining it with random noise.

"Order tends to emerge out of chaos under a very small influence," Tom said. "We think stochastic resonance in the transistor junction is the operative function for putting the voices there, but we don't know for sure."

The kinds of equipment that the AA-EVP recommends for obtaining EVP are pretty open, though they do have some suggestions depending on your equipment. "If it's a cassette recorder, then use an external microphone," Tom said. "If it's an IC recorder, then you don't need to use an external microphone, but you will need a computer to work with the sound files."

"Who thought to use the IC recorders?" I asked.

"The ghost hunters started using them first, as far as we can tell, and they worked," Tom said. "They got a lot of EVP. If they had started using cassettes, they probably would not have gotten as many EVP and probably wouldn't have gone as far as they have today with this. The IC recorder—they're really noisy inside. If you have a real high-quality recorder, like a reel-to-reel, we really recommend that you provide background noise."

"White noise," Lisa said.

"With the IC recorders, they're so noisy inside that you don't have to do that," Tom said.

Adding white noise such as a running fan, running water, or setting a radio or television to a station that doesn't come in so you get the hiss in the background of your recording is something that is a bit polarizing among paranormal investigators. "I don't use white noise, because you get enough crap in a recording that you have to pick out first anyway," said Brian Leffler, founder of the Northern Minnesota Paranormal Investigators. "The more background shifting and noise that I have to fight with, the harder it makes it for me. I try to get rid of the noise. That's the way I do it."

The AA-EVP's members are doing a host of different things with EVP—they're trying to prove, explain, or even disprove the phenomena. Tom Butler described one particularly skeptical academic member who joined their organization. "He insisted that, if these entities are real, they should be able to answer you when you ask them to do something," Tom said. "The member said, 'So I want you to record for me them saying "Mary had a little lamb."' Everybody just kind of groaned at him and said you can't make these people [spirits] do what you want them to do. But sure enough, it was about a week or two weeks later when somebody came up with a very convincing EVP of Mary had a little lamb."

"The first words ever recorded by Edison on his phonograph!" I said.

"Edison probably would have had an EVP on there if he knew to look," Tom said.

Although funny, Tom's statement brings up a point: Where should you go to get EVP? Edison's laboratory? Do you need to be in a cemetery or an allegedly haunted place to get results? The skeptics might also ask, if you really control all of the outside influences, can you still get results? The answer seems to be yes.

The same skeptical member who had asked for a nursery rhyme on demand put other controls into his own experiment. He was trying to make contact with his wife, who had passed on. Being a skeptic, he wanted to be positive that nothing could influence the audio on the recording. "He finally reached his wife by putting his recorder in a paint can and burying it out in the desert," Tom said. "And he finally got an EVP from his wife. So he was happy."

"When it happens to me"—that's the very moment that skeptics become believers. When you take a recording device out and try to make contact with a lost loved one and you recognize the voice—something that defies all logic—you become a believer. EVP has been tested in laboratories and by amateurs around the globe.

Tom Butler explained how some researchers have gone into shielded rooms within laboratories that block out all external electromagnetic radiation—which includes television, radio, cellular signals, and the like—and they still manage to record EVP, even in the electromagnetic vacuum.

If spirits aren't intervening in some of these recordings, and if external signals can be ruled out, then what else could explain EVP? There are more theories. One states that we—the living beings holding the recording device—are actually imprinting the voices onto the recorder, which obviously would still make it a heck of a phenomena, to say the least. Or maybe we're the channel and the recording device is the focusing tool for our psychic energy/influence? EVP still remains a mystery—but a mystery that people within the AA-EVP and even parts of the scientific community are actively testing.

In January of 2005, EVP went Hollywood when Universal Pictures released *White Noise*, starring Michael Keaton as architect Jonathan Rivers. In the film, Rivers loses his wife, Anna, and is soon approached by a strange man who claims she has made contact with him through EVP. Later, Rivers himself becomes obsessed with the practice and begins getting his own results through recording white noise on televisions. Most of the movie is pure Hollywood fiction, though there are a few accuracies worth pointing out. Some people do in fact become obsessed, not just with EVP but with spirit communication in general. I have known people who have become addicted to the rush of making what they believe to be contact to the point where they withdraw from living. This isn't good. What begins as part of personal grief counseling or even mild curiosity can in fact grow into something deeper—this is where the true danger of EVP lies. This is also where working within a group structure can help keep you well grounded. Another accurate portrayal in the movie are the actual "EVP" recordings—choppy, many times difficult to understand, and very brief. This is how all of the EVP I have ever heard have sounded. The movie does inaccurately blur the line between Electronic Voice Phenomenon and Instrumental Transcommunication, and for the sake of the story, they certainly make the practice appear dangerous.

One tremendous boon the film did provide was helping to bring subjects such as EVP into the mainstream. Universal spent a significant amount of time and money marketing the movie to supernatural enthusiasts. The movie trailer and television commercial content focused on explaining what EVP is as opposed to trying to hook us into the story line. This was done because having a basic understanding of EVP is critical to the film's plot. *White Noise* started some supernatural discussions on a larger scale and demonstrated the increasing accessibility of spirit communication to the general public.

Just about everyone has some kind of recording device at home, and even if they don't, recorders that will work for EVP aren't necessarily that expensive. The IC recorders—also known as digital note takers—can cost anywhere from around $35 to

$150, depending on the manufacturer and features. Reel-to-reel recorders are more difficult to find today because they're basically obsolete. Cassette recorders can cost less than $20.

"So how do I get started?" I asked the Butlers.

"Speak out loud, saying that you are about to record and that you wish the unseen entities around you to speak into the recorder," Lisa said. "Turn on the recorder and wait about 15 seconds, then speaking out loud, say where you are and ask a question. You might ask for the name of who is with you, or if they lived there in life. You can call on a loved one as well. Avoid questions with yes or no answers and allow time between each question for them to answer. Keep the recording down to two or three minutes. In the end, tell them thank you and that you are about to turn off the recorder. Wait about 15 seconds and turn off the recorder."

The Butlers suggest playing the recording back in short segments so you can concentrate and look for anomalies with voice-like qualities. There are recording devices and software packages that allow you to speed up and slow down the recording to listen for subtle noise. EVP takes some practice—both on the recording and listening sides of the equation.

For my own EVP experiments, I picked up an Olympus Digital Voice Recorder (VN-240PC). The device enables me to play back through the external speaker or headphones, or I can then download the files to my computer to explore them with more advanced software.

I took the recorder out to my back deck. The deck is about 8 feet from the ground and about 25 feet from the woods, where many large pine trees line

My digital recorder—used for attempting EVP in my backyard. Photo by Jeff Belanger.

the edge of my yard. I also have two hanging birdfeeders nearby. I stood in the corner of my deck and held the recorder. "I'm going to record for one minute," I announced. "If anyone can hear me, please speak your name into the recorder."

Throughout the minute of recording, I made two other statements. "If you can hear me, you have 30 seconds left to make contact," I said, and then, "I'm turning off the recorder in 15 seconds. Please speak into the recorder if you wish to communicate."

During the outside recording, there was a lot of wind whooshing through the pines. Birds peeped and squawked as well. A titmouse and chickadee even flew up to the birdfeeder that was located 3 feet from where I was standing—apparently they were more hungry than frightened.

I then played the recording back through headphones. I heard the rushing wind, the singing birds, and my own voice very clearly. But I didn't hear anything unusual.

I repeated my experiment in my kitchen. (I know I promised my wife I wouldn't conduct these experiments in the house, but she wasn't home. So please don't tell her.) This time I let the water run from my sink faucet during the recording to add background noise. I recorded for one minute and again announced how much time was left.

When I played this recording back, I was surprised at how metallic the running water sounded. I may have held my recorder too close to the water. I heard my voice—though it was almost drowned out (pun intended) by the water. But no anomalous sounds.

One thing did happen during the second recording process, and the recording can confirm this. I had the water running pretty close to full-blast. This time I said, "Can you give me a sign that you hear me?" during the recording, and the strength of the water force immediately slowed, until I completed the recording; I found the timing interesting.

EVP Classifications

AA-EVP Founder Sarah Estep came up with the following EVP grading system:

- ❧ **Class A**: The message can be heard without headphones and people generally agree on which words were spoken.
- ❧ **Class B**: Usually requires listening through headphones to discern the message content and not everyone will agree on which words were spoken.
- ❧ **Class C**: Requires headphones, may need amplification and filtering, and the words may still not be discernable.

EVP Examples

> Note: You can listen to the three EVP recordings discussed in the following section by visiting *www.ghostvillage.com/spiritcommunication*.

RECORDED BY: Brian Leffler

LOCATION: Private Residence in Cohasset, Minnesota

DATE: September 2003

Brian Leffler is the founder of the Northern Minnesota Paranormal Investigators, or NMPI (*www.nmpi-scary.com*). He and his group were investigating a private residence rented by a member's niece, named Ashley, and her boyfriend, Dave. "We investigated the house because Ashley had a few strange things going on," Leffler said. "Her lights would go off or on and her cats would go crazy at 'nothing.' She and Dave were very skeptical about the whole ghost thing to begin with, so they had us come out."

NMPI brought some of their standard equipment with them on the investigation, including several recorders, 35mm cameras, a video camera, Electromagnetic Field (EMF) Meter, and an infrared thermometer. Leffler explained how it is standard practice for his group to have multiple recorders going during the investigation. For this recording, he used a GE microcassette recorder with a remote mic and Sony tapes. He points out that he always uses a new, blank tape when trying to record EVP to ensure he's not hearing something residual on the tape. This is why Leffler also prefers cassettes to digital, because he knows computer chips can never be wiped completely clean, and using a blank memory chip each time isn't financially practical.

In the audio clip, you can clearly hear Leffler in the beginning saying, "We'll be telling them that they're bound here." Next, a very clear and whispering male voice comes in and says, "We are bound here now. We aren't going anywhere."

Hearing this voice takes no imagination at all. In fact, the second voice is clearer than Brian Leffler's voice on the tape— almost as if the entity got close to the microphone to speak. What is profound is that the voice is not only clear, but it responds intelligently to what was being said. Leffler was explaining to his group how, as a matter of protocol, they tell the spirits they are bound to the location, to prevent anything supernatural from attaching itself to the investigators and following them home. The spirit voice responded to that comment. The chances of picking up a stray radio or cell phone signal that would say those words at that instant seems extremely remote.

RECORDED BY: Melanie Billings
LOCATION: Piedmont, South Carolina
DATE: November 2004

Melanie Billings is an independent paranormal researcher and also a member of the AA-EVP. She began experimenting with her Sony ICD-P17 IC recorder in her home in 2004. "I wouldn't say my house is haunted exactly," Billings said, "but I do have the sense that something passes through every now and again. We have experienced mild poltergeist activity that seems to come and go every few weeks. Things disappear and reappear in odd places, objects fling themselves off shelves in our bathroom, we've smelled odd, out-of-place smells (such as cigar smoke), heard footsteps, heard knocks on the walls, seen a stray orb here and there, and on two occasions my husband felt a hand on his back while he was in bed alone."

Not exactly haunted? With activity like that, who needs hauntings, right?

Billings has been researching ghosts and the paranormal for several years. She finally tried obtaining EVP for herself after she had the opportunity to interview Tom and Lisa Butler of the AA-EVP for a paranormal Website she was writing for at the time. "After trying it, I was hooked," she said. "I continue to be absolutely fascinated with it, and I think what's most intriguing is the fact that the voices seem to actually answer questions asked them time and time again, under all sorts of different circumstances and conditions. These are audible and intelligible words being formed out of thin air in direct response to a question—if they aren't the disembodied voices of people on the other side, then what are they?"

In November of 2004, Billings recorded a clip in her kitchen with her IC recorder. When she played it back, she heard a deep, staccato-voiced man say, "Shut the hell up," though I believe it's possible the voice is using a stronger expletive than "hell."

"This one spooked me a bit and made a believer out of my husband, who was in the house at the time I made the recording," Billings said. "He is a die-hard skeptic, and when he heard the voice coming from the recording I had made just minutes before, he was hard-pressed to find an explanation for it. It has tone and inflection exactly as a real voice would but still has that strange, flat EVP quality to it. We call it the 'grumpy old man' because that's exactly what it sounds like. I haven't encountered this grumpy old man since then, thankfully."

RECORDED BY: Coby Baldauf
LOCATION: Bergen County, New Jersey
DATE: April 20, 2003

Coby Baldauf is the founder of the Connecticut Paranormal Research Team (*www.ctprt.org*) and has been studying the supernatural his entire life—considering he grew up in a haunted farmhouse in Bergen County, New Jersey. The house was built in 1863 and is still owned by his family. While living there as a child and young adult, Baldauf experienced shadowy figures crisscrossing the rooms of the home, banging sounds, and footsteps. On an Easter visit in 2003, he brought along his ghost investigating equipment. His recording equipment consisted of the following: a Philips AQ6341 Memo Recorder with Voice Activation, a Labtec Verse-504 Microphone, a Radio Shack DR-90 Digital Recorder, and a Radio Shack HC-60, 60 minute High Bias Type II cassette tape.

On Friday, he set up both digital and analog recording equipment in the house. The digital was set on voice-activation so any sounds would cause the device to start recording.

"I was beat from the drive, so I showed my mother how to take the digital recorder off of pause so it would start recording whenever it heard a noise," Baldauf said. "I set up the recorder upstairs and then went to bed. Around 12:30 to 12:45 a.m., my mother headed off to bed and switched the recorder off of pause. As my mother is walking up the stairs, you can clearly hear a man's voice—though no one was on the main floor."

On the file Baldauf sent me, he enhanced the EVP by boosting the volume of the voice on both channels to 202 percent and nothing more. On the audio file, you can hear the footsteps and what sounds like a deep-voiced man in a loud whisper saying, "We'll never get out, the house is full."

EVP collection is growing. Whether simply curious about reaching beyond the grave, trying to receive a message to help cope with the loss of a loved one, or making EVP a standard part of a paranormal investigation, more people are open to the idea than ever before. What began early in the 20th century—but really started gaining acceptance in the last 30 years—is a profound method of spirit communication. Since humans could communicate, they used what they could to reach across to their ancestors; fire and ceremonies are being replaced by recorders and modern technology. Today, people still use the means and methods available to them to make spirit contact— our oracles now carry brand names such as Sony, General Electric, Olympus, and many others. Next time you find yourself alone, grab your favorite device and hit "record." Upon playback, you may just find that you have some company.

" I began to search for spiritual understanding, which I never cared about before.
I wanted some kind of evidential information, not just something based on faith and belief. "

Instrumental Transcommunication

I'm definitely a technology buff. As a child, when I was given mechanical and electronic toys, one of my first priorities was to take them apart. I remember sitting in my friend Steven's basement in Lewisburg, Pennsylvania. We were dismantling a remote control car of his, and as we tinkered with moving the wires around the circuit board, we heard a man's voice say a few words. I don't recall what the words were, but it was clearly a man's voice. The funny thing is that the car didn't have a speaker in it. But I know the sounds came out of those circuits, wires, and plastic because we both heard it.

Instrumental Transcommunication (ITC) is the practice of using technology to make contact with the spirit world. The birth of ITC coincides with the birth of modern technology and with the Spiritualist movement. As we've seen in previous chapters, just a few years after the camera was invented, people began using it for spirit contact. Thomas Edison as well as many other noted scientists were trying to study supernatural phenomena; they took the position: *If this is for real, then it can be measured. We simply need to develop the tools and systems to be able to touch it.*

Electronic Voice Phenomena (EVP) is a subset or kind of precursor to ITC. In fact, you could say EVP was what started it all. As soon as recording equipment became accessible to the masses, people began to explore its esoteric uses. Devices used in ITC today include radios, tape recorders, televisions, telephones, fax machines, answering machines, video cameras, and even computers, to capture audio, images, and text from beyond.

As the now-famous story goes, the first telephone call took place March 6, 1876, when Alexander Graham Bell used his new device to call to his assistant in another room. "Come here, Watson, I want you" were the first words uttered through the telephone. About half a century later, Bell's invention was adapted to communicate even further than across states, countries, or oceans—some people were claiming to use the phone to reach the afterlife. In 1925, Oscar d'Argonell wrote *Voices from Beyond by Telephone*, an account of his telephone conversations with spirit friends. Allegedly, the voices gave the Brazilian author many facts that he was later able to verify that proved he was indeed talking with someone who had passed on.

Can you imagine receiving a long-distance phone call from a friend...who died years ago? D'Argonell isn't the only person to make the claim. Even today some say they experience these calls.

Like all branches of scientific study, ITC evolved over many years of successes and failures. We've already covered much of ITC's earliest history in regards to Edison and then EVP. This chapter focuses on more recent history.

ITC as we know it today got its start in the late 1970s. Not surprisingly, this was when film and video cameras, home computers, and other recording devices were becoming more accessible to regular people.

One of the early pioneers of ITC was George W. Meek, who conducted extensive testing and development of spirit communication devices intended to enable a simple, two-way dialogue between a spirit and a living person. Meek postulated that spirit energy is not a part of the electromagnetic spectrum as we know it. To detect or interact with spirits, it was essential to create a way to couple spirit energies with our technology, and he believed something like a transducer was necessary to be the technical interface between their energies and ours.

In 1979, Meek's "Spiricom" device was built to be a sort of "walkie-talkie" to beyond. The machine was comprised of tone and frequency generators that emitted 13 tones in the range of an adult man's voice. When Meek spoke to the spirit world through his machine, the spirit world spoke back by interacting with the tone generators to make recognizable speech. Meek was astounded at his breakthrough.

The spirit voice coming through Spiricom identified itself as that of Dr. George Jeffries Mueller, a former NASA scientist and university professor who had died in 1967. The spirit of Dr. Mueller said he had come close to Earth to communicate with Meek, but not only communicate—to help him further develop the machine. He would be Meek's spirit colleague.

Meek recorded more than 20 hours of audio communication with Dr. Mueller through the Spiricom device. On the World ITC Association Website (www.worlditc.org), there is an audio file where you can hear a piece of the conversation in which Mueller offers specific technical direction on how to improve the machine. "I think that can be corrected by introducing a 150-ohm, half-watt resistor in parallel..." you can hear the voice say if you listen very closely. In the audio clip, Meek's voice is clear; the mechanized spirit voice sounds similar to the speech system used by Stephen Hawking, only Mueller's is significantly closer to a monotone voice and has no inflection. Meek claimed that his spirit colleague's feedback and suggestions were a critical part of development.

After December 1981, Meek was no longer able to receive communications through Spiricom. One explanation offered was that his main contact on the other side, Doc Mueller, had gone on to a higher plane and no longer wished to make contact through the machine. But Meek claimed to have had contact with other people besides Mueller during the two years of Spiricom's operation; those people could no longer be reached either. This created obvious controversy in the spring of 1982, when word of Meek's machine spread. The results couldn't be reproduced. According to J.G. Fuller's book *The Ghost of 29 Megacycles*, Meek sent out Spiricom's schematics to several hundred technicians around the world. No one has been able to reproduce the results. The original Spiricom machine was allegedly dismantled and its parts now reside with multiple colleagues of Meek.

Considering the length, specificity, and nature of his conversations through Spiricom, Meek believed with certainty that he was successful in making controlled and regular contact. In 1988, he penned the book *After We Die, What Then?*, a work that greatly furthered the spirit communication discussion. He wrote, "For the first time in 8,000 years of recorded history, it can now be said with certainty that our mind, memory, personality, and soul will survive physical death."

George Meek died in 1999, though many still continue the work in ITC that he helped pioneer.

In 1984, spirit messages apparently began appearing on computer screens. Ken Webster's 1990 book, *The Vertical Plane*, details some of the hundreds of messages he received on his computer between 1984 and 1985 from Thomas Harden—a 16th-century Englishman who once owned Webster's house in Dodleston, England. The computer was an old word processor with 32 kilobytes of memory and no hard drive, meaning files had to be saved on 5.25-inch floppy disks. What was first dismissed as a prank evolved into Webster's belief that there was truly something supernatural going on. Webster would come home to find messages on the monitor—or "light box," as the spirit of Harden referred to the machine. In these communications, Harden wrote in an old English dialect and stated that Webster was living in *his* house.

Around this time, other ITC explorers were experimenting with ideas such as filming feedback loops on televisions. This is done by taking a video camera, plugging it into a television so the television is showing what the camera sees, and then pointing the camera at the television, which causes video feedback—a series of jumping frames, static that fades in and out, and seemingly random patterns that form the visual "noise." This feedback is then recorded. During playback, especially at slow speeds or when viewing the images frame by frame, some researchers have found that the patterns become recognizable—sometimes human shapes form; in the most profound cases, the human is instantly recognizable as someone the researcher knew in life.

Our technology is developing so quickly today that the scope of ITC is limited only by our imaginations. But considering the amount of technology we now have, we also have to be twice as vigilant in ruling out false positives. AM, FM, satellite transmissions, cellular, short wave, CB, and a host of other electromagnetic signals are circling all around us, and software and computer operating systems are rushed to market with bugs that can cause anomalies in performance. To judge the validity of the message, we must examine the content.

If a computer spits out some random numbers, that may very well be a computer hiccup (or even a virus). To see a message with significant meaning to its reader that references memories, situations, and anecdotes from our lives or the lives of our deceased loved ones, well, that deserves a closer look.

In my last book, *The World's Most Haunted Places*, I interviewed Sharon Helfrich, the director of the Andrew Bayne Memorial Library in Pittsburgh, Pennsylvania. The ghost of Amanda Bayne Balph has been seen on occasion around the library for several years. One of the phenomena the staff has reported include anomalies with the library's computer system. Numbers have occasionally popped up on the screen for no apparent reason. "I would be standing at the charge desk computer and then a number would scan on the computer behind me, and no one was anywhere near that computer," Helfrich said. "I'd hear 'beep,' and a number would come up. We've tried to play some of the numbers she's flashed onto the computer in the lottery, and it never really hits. We love her [Amanda] dearly, but she's not real lucky."

A random computer glitch or attempted spirit contact through ITC?

For a better understanding of ITC, I spoke with Mark Macy, author of *Miracles in the Storm: Talking to the Other Side With the New Technology of Spiritual Contact*, cofounder of the World ITC Association, and a founding member of the now-dormant International Network for Instrumental Transcommunication (INIT). According to its mission statement, the objective of the World ITC Association is to promote decency in human relationships, to sustain resonance among ITC researchers, and to forge a link with the light, ethereal realms of existence.

Macy spoke with me from his home outside of Boulder, Colorado. The 55-year-old former atheist began exploring ITC around 1988 after he was diagnosed with colon cancer. "I began to search for spiritual understanding, which I never cared about before," he said. "I wanted some kind of evidential information, not just something based on faith and belief."

One of the biggest draws of spirit communication devices is the tangible evidence of contact that's so difficult to find in many organized religions. Macy's motivation for seeking spirit communication is similar to that of many others: to know there's an afterlife.

"What happened next?" I asked.

"I ran into George Meek, and he introduced me to the experts in Europe such as the Harsch-Fischbach couple." Jules Harsch and Maggy Harsch-Fischbach were Luxembourg-based ITC experimenters who got their start making spirit contact through radio systems in 1985.

"I went to meet with them a couple of times," Macy said. "We had some amazing contacts through radio, and we established an international group called INIT. From that association, I began to get some amazing contacts of my own." These contacts quickly dissolved Macy's atheism.

ITC involves teams and equipment—on both sides of the veil—operating on a higher state of consciousness. What separates ITC from other forms of spirit communication, such as EVP, is the two-way dialogue with a higher realm. Macy explained how EVP involves spirits who are either closer to the earth already, meaning they exist in a lower astral plane, or spirits from a higher plane who venture close to the earth to somehow imprint their voices onto the recording device. But consistent dialogue requires an advanced frame of mind and ITC.

ITC is about communicating with spirits we would not normally have the opportunity to communicate with. According to modern understanding within the ITC community, spirits we refer to as "ghosts" are the earthbound variety. These are the kinds of entities that may respond to communication methods such as talking boards, EVP, spirit photography, and the like. That's not to say only the lower earthbound spirits make contact via these methods, just that they're more likely to.

Macy also explained how only beings on the higher planes are capable of organizing into groups and creating an apparatus to work with devices in our world to facilitate communication.

"There are teams of specific spirits on the other side working with teams of people on this side, and through that ongoing inter-action, a contact field develops between our world and their world," he said. "The contact field is what allows these more enhanced contacts through telephone, computer, radio, and that kind of thing. And it's usually assisted by ethereal beings who have tremendous power to manifest all sorts of things between dimensions."

This was the first I'd ever heard of physical mechanisms in the spirit world. Macy explained how the team on the other side has some kind of spirit apparatus that interfaces directly with our devices. Imagine an ethereal machine that fits on top of our radios, telephones, or computers to bridge the gap between the two worlds.

I consider myself to have a better-than-average understand-ing of computers and how they work. I know how viruses, severely fragmented hard drives, and corrupted software can cause strange goings-on within your computer. But having files appear on the hard drive with images of deceased people whom you or your colleagues knew in life is definitely beyond the reach of random chance. Macy said, "A couple had left their home to go to work. They made sure everything was turned off. The spirit team from the other side would come into their apartment, somehow turn on the computer, and plant new files on the disk. The files contained actual pictures of life on the other side. Those were by far the most astounding pictures I've ever seen from the other side when we were getting them. But that finished up around the year 2000 when personalities got involved and ruined the contact field."

One of the pictures Macy described is available on the World ITC Website and depicts George Meek's late wife, Jeannette, standing in front a beautiful landscape with rolling hills in the background, a calm body of water, and lush flora in the foreground.

To reach these spirits in the higher astral levels—the place that we may refer to as heaven, Summerland, or the higher realm—takes support on many levels.

"How do you get the cooperation with the other side?" I asked.

"Through meditation and purity of thought," Macy said. "One thing they've [the spirits] talked about is that they are always in a joyous state of mind. On Earth, we kind of go up and down and have a roller-coaster ride every day throughout our lives. We get angry, we get delighted about things—it's easier for them [the spirits] to align with us if we can maximize that joy within us."

"You mean on a personal level?" I asked.

"On an interpersonal level, especially. If you've got a group of people who are working together, if they're mostly trusting and loving and friendly with each other, it becomes very natural for the types of people we need on the other side to come in close and work with us through ITC.

"If there are doubts, fears, jealousies, and animosities among the people, then it becomes easier for the darker, more troubled spirits that are closer to the earth to kind of move in, and they have no organization, no ability to create the ITC contacts. We want the people who are in this joyous state, who have the organization and the collaboration with each other—the warm feelings with each other already—working with other people on Earth who also have those warm feelings that keep us close. That's the key to ITC—in a nutshell, that's it."

Macy has made his own contribution to ITC with Polaroid photography and a Luminator—a mechanism developed by Patrick Richards. The device stands about 4 feet tall and looks kind of like a speaker tower. Inside the Luminator are two fans that move air over several liquid-filled rings. The machine's inventor claims the air molecule movement over the rings causes the electrons to spin in reverse—the area in a 100-foot radius of the operating device is altered. Macy uses the Luminator in conjunction with a Polaroid camera. He takes photographs of people, and when the image develops on the instant paper, many times the subject's face may appear as a blur. Within the blur, another face may make an appearance. The face of a spirit.

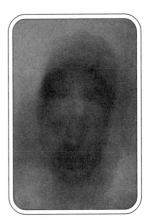

In 2000, Macy took a series of Polaroid photographs of his then-14-year-old son, Aaron, in the presence of the Luminator. The first picture has no anomalies, while the second photo and especially the third show a new face that Aaron didn't recognize, but that his mother immediately did. "That's my father!" his mom said. Aaron's grandfather had died three years before he was born. The bottom photo shows Aaron's mother and grandfather in 1953. Macy claims these ITC images have given his son a closer bond with the grandfather he never knew in life. Photos courtesy of Mark Macy.

Since 2000, INIT has been inactive and the communication they were receiving has ceased because the dynamic of the group had shifted. Today, Macy is involved with a small group within the World ITC Association called the Resonance Working Group (RWG). He and about a dozen other colleagues from around the world are trying to create the contact field needed to open up dialogue with a group on the other side again. Today, they're using message boards on the Internet to share information—significantly streamlining their cooperation compared with the physical meetings, faxes, phone calls, and postal correspondence that were necessary to hold a multi-continental group such as that together. I asked if they had achieved any spirit contact through their Web-based message boards. "Not yet," Macy told me.

I asked because, on Ghostvillage.com, we had an interesting experience with a person who posted on our message boards and claimed to be a spirit. I have very little doubt that this was an actual living person pulling a prank, but a few of our members played along and asked some questions about what it was like on the other side.

"The way I understand it," Macy said, "it would be difficult for spirits to come through on a larger public forum because of the different attitudes and beliefs that would cause a very cloudy contact field."

Timestream Spirit Group is a team in the spirit world with whom Macy and his INIT colleagues have made contact. Timestream made contact through radio, video, fax, computer, and telephone. Macy says he received several spirit phone calls during the peak of the INIT group.

"How does it work?" I asked. "The phone rings, and you answer it?" (*I know, great question, Jeff. Am I a journalist or what?*)

"Exactly. It happens just like a regular telephone call, except the voice sounds a little bit more artificial. Timestream, the spirit team we worked with, they set up proofs."

"You mean like a way to validate that the connection with a spirit was real?" I asked.

"Right. Phone calls can easily be faked from this side because it's through a public network. We find that with the spirit phone calls, they can't be traced. There's no record from the phone company that these phone calls ever happened. It's like they [the spirit team] establish their equipment right over ours and they don't go through the public network to make these contacts."

"What happened with the phone calls you received?"

"I would get a phone call on one day," he said. "And then the next day, a fellow in Germany whom I had never met, but who was also an ITC researcher and involved in this work, would get a computer contact saying 'We herewith confirm our contact with Macy in the States. This is Konstantin Raudive.' That cross-contact is very helpful in verifying the legitimacy of the contact."

"Did you recognize the voice on the phone as someone you knew in life?"

"Not through the telephone. The telephone calls I got were all from Konstantin Raudive—he was a pioneer in this work before he died, and he became a key player in Timestream on the other side after he died. I guess it was difficult for them [the spirits] to create apparatuses for each person to convey their information. So apparently they used him a lot for contacts with a lot of people."

Where there's a phone, many times there's also an answering machine. In April of 1999, Margaret Houck of Knoxville, Iowa, had an unintentional encounter with ITC. She first contacted me about her experience in June 2004. "I received a message on my answering machine a few months after my father passed," Houck said. "The night the message was left, I needed to pick up someone by 5:15 p.m., so I left at 5:00 p.m. The recording occurred at 5:15. If I had been home, I would have probably hung up the phone and it wouldn't have been recorded."

Houck described how she was in such deep mourning after her father passed away that she sobbed at night until her back would arch up off the bed. Houck is a registered nurse, so dealing with death is not something new to her, but she admits that, when it was her father, it was different.

"When I listened to the message several times, I could smell his distinct body scent," she said. "Sometime later, my door chime began playing the Westminster chimes, which it is incapable of doing. My dad was a jokester! He had my husband and I running all over the house trying to figure it out. My husband kept pushing the doorbell to try and make it do it again, but it only happened when Dad wanted to have some fun."

The audio starts with the answering machine announcing, "You have one message" followed by 35 seconds of strange sounds. There's some hissing, muted tones, and beeps that almost sound like they're underwater, and the sounds repeatedly fade in and fade out. It sounds nothing like when a cellular phone cuts in and out, and it's not like anything I've personally ever heard through a phone before. I could not make out any voices in the segment. Houck, though, believes she hears something, "I hear many words," she said. "He [my dad] starts off trying to say my name—Ma...Ma...Margaret, I love you, Margie. I'm with Grandpa and Grandma. Do not call Lene [Darlene, her younger sister] or anyone else...Try not to worry about anyone else dying...try!"

The proof, especially for Houck, is her feeling when she heard the message. Maybe this message was only meant for her, and that's why she can hear it. She said, "I know I hear his voice under the 'wet' sounds, but others are dumbfounded by the recording—they can't hear a voice. I believe that my father had to use a lot of energy just so he could call and comfort me that he is still around. Of course I miss him still, but I talk to him as if he is right next to me. He proved to me that he does still exist."

Since April of 1999, Houck moved to Van Buren, Arkansas, and claims her family is still receiving the occasional phone call from her father. "My grandson, Skylar, was talking on the phone with a classmate," Houck said. "He began hearing the same "squooshy" sounds that I had on my recording. He started listening and heard a man say in a monotone voice, 'I've been trying to call...I love you.' My daughter and I told him it was Grandpa Wallace."

In Margaret Houck's case, she wasn't trying to create contact—she simply feels her father reached out to her because she needed to hear from him. Or maybe her father felt he needed to reach out to his family. The end result was the same: Houck was comforted knowing her father was still around based on these telephone experiences.

For steady spirit contact, I gathered from my discussion with Mark Macy that the more serious and committed the individual or team is on this side, the more resources will be committed on the other side.

ITC also requires a faith that needs to run a little deeper than with some of the other devices and methods we've discussed in this book. With tarot cards, for example, you may get a message through the cards, and whether that message came from the spirit world or random luck may not matter. The message itself is what's important. With ITC, you need to believe that there are beings on the other side waiting to make the connection with you through these cooperative systems.

For my own ITC experimentation, Macy suggested I use the equipment I have—whether that be a radio and recording device, video, or computer. "Just keep working for the voices and contact," he said. "Be aware of your friends on the other side, even though you don't know who they are exactly in the beginning. Just be aware of their presence, and eventually a rapport develops."

Video ITC has intrigued me since I first learned about it from a television program years ago. I have a JVC digital video camera that I don't use nearly enough, so I took an unused videotape and set up my tripod about 3 feet in front of my television. I checked the reflection on the TV screen and turned off a lamp that was casting a glare onto the screen. Once the room was set, I connected the camera to the television and saw that everything was working.

At this point, I put the lens cap back on and just listened. The house was perfectly quiet. "I'm trying to establish contact," I announced. "I'm going to film for 45 seconds. If anyone wants to come through, now is the time." Popping the lens cap off, I focused on the television set, which revealed many pictures within pictures of the TV. I zoomed in past the frame of the television—the image was like moving through a tunnel to a bright light waiting on the other side. Once the camera was focused on only the screen and its own image, the screen went blue for a moment before the feedback started. The screen flashed white, then went through a series of various waves, jumps, skips, blue flashes, and more white flashes. At certain points, the screen looked like something out of the movie *The Matrix*, when all of the visual images turn into data streams. I heard feedback through the speakers of the television so I lowered the volume to zero. In this experiment, I wanted video feedback only.

I filmed and watched the screen, intently looking for some kind of sign that a higher being was reaching out to me. The jumping patterns were mesmerizing. They changed, steadied, popped, and rolled with no regularity. Once the feedback started, I expected to see a consistent pattern, but I didn't. After 45 seconds, I stopped the recording, rewound the tape, and watched the feedback all the way through again without stopping. Again, nothing popped out at me as a potential contact, so I rewound again, but this time I used a feature that allowed me to advance the video one frame at a time.

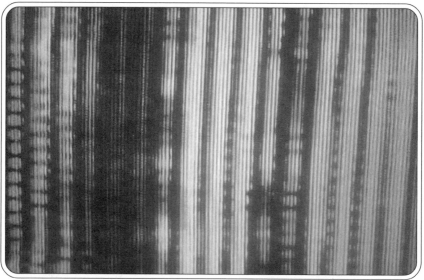

A sample of what the screen looked like during frame-by-frame playback. Photo by Jeff Belanger.

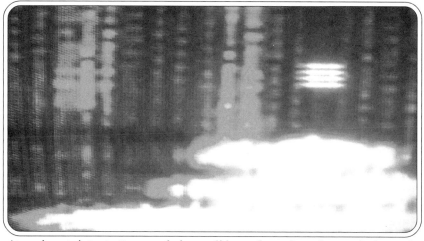

At various points, patterns and shapes did stand out from the seemingly random pattern. Photo by Jeff Belanger.

I did see a few patterns and shapes that were different than most of the other patterns, but nothing even remotely conclusive.

My friend and colleague, Dennis Lytle, of the Website *www.PhantomsInTheDark.com*, has also done some experiments with video feedback ITC. I spoke to him from his office in Saginaw, Michigan, about the results he got in his basement in the early fall of 2004.

The basement of his home has a history of paranormal activity. He told me how lights would turn on and off by themselves while he was down there. On one occasion he even gave a lecture to this presence in his basement—he explained how rude it is to turn the lights out on him when he is in the basement. Lytle's lecture was answered with the lights turning out again.

Lytle, a former science teacher, was spurned to try his first ITC experiment when he sensed a strong presence in his basement one day. He set up his video camera in front of the television screen and began to record. "Once I started the recording process, I turned the lights out," Lytle said. "And by doing that, you're taking the light that's actually on the

TV screen and you end up with a pulsing effect where that actual light is captured and recycled over and over without any extraneous interference from other light. So there is nothing there except for this light that's pulsing on it. And then there's what I would call this super amplification of that same light—you can hold it for maybe 10 to 15 seconds and then you lose it."

"So there's a diminishing return on the amount of light and the size of the pulsing effect?" I asked.

"Right. Just a few seconds is all you get. And when you're reviewing the footage frame by frame, a few seconds is all you really want to look at anyway."

In reviewing each frame of his footage, that's when Lytle made his discovery. "I captured something strange there," he said.

Dennis Lytle's video ITC results. The camera's infrared emitters were turned off; the image only shows recycled light in total darkness. Photo by Dennis Lytle.

"I know it's open to interpretation," he said, "but what I saw on the picture was like you are laying in a field surrounded by trees and looking up at three figures. And there also seems to be a wolf in one of the amplified pictures. The results and the presence I felt was overpowering—so strong—so I just backed off."

"So you haven't pursued any further ITC experiments since?" I asked.

"No. You're not much of a researcher when you back off, I know. I backed off to think about it a little bit."

I also asked Mark Macy if he had ever tried the video feedback method of ITC. "I tried that once or twice, but it's not something that resonated with me personally," he said.

The concept of "resonance" is a common theme with Macy. There are many definitions of resonance—some relate to acoustics and involve prolonged tones produced by sympathetic vibrations. The physics definition involves detecting subatomic particles that exist for too short of a time period to be observed directly. In regards to ITC, it's the vibration or echo we humans give of in response to an otherworldly stimulus. It's almost a cliché in psychic circles to discuss "sensing the vibrations," but that's the same thing ITC attempts to detect and turn into images, audio, and/or text.

Macy and I spoke about our human tendency toward pattern recognition—finding human features and faces in patterns, as was discussed in the spirit photography chapter. And skeptics of this practice have a host of valid questions: How do you know your equipment isn't picking up stray signals? Do you have an old television that may have images slightly burned into the screen from prolonged use? Was your tape completely blank when you started recording? And many others.

"How do you know if you have a genuine video contact?" I asked Macy.

"If the image on the TV screen develops over a period of many frames into something that's very obvious like a human face and it lasts for many frames before it disappears, that's pretty evidential to me," he said. "But if it's just one or two frames that happen to show a pattern—that could be just random noise—that's just coincidence, I think."

Paranormal research groups are increasingly adding techniques such as ITC to the tools they use in haunted location investigations. Considering how many paranormal research groups are popping up all over the world all of the time, I asked Macy if he had any advice for these groups to help improve the evidence and quality of results they may be getting.

"Rather than go to haunted places where you have maybe one or two troubled spirits hanging out over a period of many years, kind of trapped near the earth," he said, "establish a place in your own home where you bring the good kind of spirits who you want to have a connection with. Start developing a team effort from both sides of the veil with that spirit group—that's how you establish ITC rapport."

Technology continues to improve in speed and efficiency, decrease in cost, and become more engrained in our culture and lives. But ITC doesn't offer the promise of an instant connection with the spirit world just because technology is involved. And the latest and greatest technology isn't required either. But like all other spirit communication techniques, ITC requires time, dedication, and patience. But the reward is significant: ITC offers proof, even if only for the person who made the capture. A video, photograph, or sound recording is something you can experience again and again in the future. ITC offers more than a fleeting moment with the spirit world; the practice can potentially open up a two-way dialogue. The very best minds from the past may just be waiting for us to try and tune in to them.

"The runes are symbols for communication—communication between gods and men,

men and the universe, and between human beings over time and space.

The great and numerous runestones of Scandinavia are important parts of the communication

between the living and the dead."

Runes

There's something captivating about ancient symbols. Hieroglyphs, old carvings, and runes are the written language of ancient peoples. These symbols are their very voices frozen into lines and drawings. To know a language is to know a people— it's how we can truly communicate.

Written language is arguably the most important human advancement ever created. Writing makes people immortal; it means good thoughts and ideas don't disappear as soon as the person who conceived them walks away or dies. In many belief systems, the letters themselves are sacred; such is the case of runes.

Ancient Germanic dialects may differ slightly in spelling or pronunciation—rûna, rún, or rûn—but the meanings are the same: *rune* means "mystery." The exact origins of these symbols are unknown. The only account we have is one passed down through many centuries of folklore.

The runes are said to come from Odin—an Aesir god and head of the Norse pantheon. For nine days, Odin hung upside down from *Yggdrasil*, or the Tree of the World. He bled from a wound inflicted by his own sword and suffered in solitude through hunger, thirst, and pain. On the ninth day, just before he fell from the great tree, he saw the runes. With his remaining strength, he grabbed the cryptic symbols then fell. This is said to be when the characters were brought into our world, and thus, the birth of written language for the Norse people.

According to Edred Thorsson's *Runecaster's Handbook: The Well of Wyrd*, the first runes show up as early as 200 B.C.E. and were comprised of 24 symbols or staves. Today, this oldest-known group of runes is referred to as the Elder Futhark—Futhark being the first six letters of the alphabet: f-u-th-a-r-k or ᚠᚢᚦᚨᚱᚲ.

This writing system flourished until 1050 C.E., when other alphabets and languages took over, and the system died out everywhere but Scandinavia. The writing survived in small pockets but was mostly lost, save for some ancient carvings and manuscripts that we still have today. The lack of knowing the symbols' origins, meaning, and use only adds to their enigma. For many, the runes still speak to us and offer divine insight and answers even in our modern times. In his *The Book of Runes*, Ralph H. Blum wrote, "An Oracle always responds to the requirements of the time in which it is consulted—and to the needs of those consulting it."

I first looked at runes about a year before this writing. A friend spilled a bag of these symbols out on the table in front of me. It was a set he created by painting the symbols with red paint onto tiny animal bones. I found my first glance confusing—the many lines and shapes blurred into a mess. When I began my rune research for this book, I bought my own set and I took the stones and studied each symbol one at a time. I've read some books where the runecasters say they meditated on each rune until it spoke to them. My initial study wasn't nearly as complex or profound. I just looked, turned the stone around, followed the lines of the symbol with my eyes or finger, then moved on to the next. These symbols do beg us to look deeper. And in looking deeper, we learn how to use them.

The study of runes is a lesson in solitude. There are books, other runecasters, and even rune organizations that can teach you more, but the breakthroughs happen alone, when you come to your own understanding.

Many runecasters recommend creating your own set of runes because that set will mean more to you compared with something you buy. You can create runes by painting the symbols on rocks, pieces of wood, sticks, bones, plastic, or even on pieces of paper or note cards. Some books on runes recommend an elaborate ceremony for creating each rune—some suggest creating one per day so you can focus all of your energy and intent on each piece. Likewise, storing them should also be conducted in a respectful manner, whether it be in a box or bag, as long as it has meaning to the runecaster. Like any esoteric practice, the more fortitude you put into the system, the more results you're likely to get out.

Edred Thorsson is one of the foremost experts on runes, their origins, and their use in divination and magic. He received his Ph.D. in Germanic Languages and Medieval Studies from the University of Texas and has been studying these symbols since the 1970s. In corresponding with Thorsson, I asked him how he learned about this ancient practice.

"My first introduction to the runes came in the form of a word whispered in my ear under mysterious circumstances," he said. "I was on one of those typical occult wild goose chases in 1974 and in the midst of this, I 'heard' the one word, 'runa.' I recognized this as having something to do with the ancient Germanic writing system, with which I was only barely familiar. After I heard this word, I began doing research on the runes in the academic library at the University of Texas at Austin."

"Have you drawn a conclusion as to whose voice whispered that word?" I asked.

"Without doubt this was the Old Man—Odin. Just as he whispered this word in the ear of Baldur [Norse god of beauty, purity, and peace; Odin's second son], so too does he occasionally whisper it in the ear of one here in Midgard [middle world]. The fact of this whispering is best demonstrated not in my assertion of the idea, but rather in the fruits that this whispering brought forth in my life and in the world at large in the subsequent years. It has been my experience that when a god really speaks, that god does not need to prattle on.

Rather, one word is sufficient. It has taken me a lifetime to unravel even part of the meaning of this word."

With tarot, I understand that the cards are simply a tool within a person's spirituality. The cards themselves do not represent a belief system. I asked Thorsson if the same were true for runes. "The runes are also tools in a wider philosophy," he said. "That philosophy is the Way of Odin. The runes are a complex code for inter-reality communication, both within the subjective universe of the thinker and between that universe and the wider objective universe beyond it."

Spirit communication is a primary objective of runes. When a runecaster spills his or her runes—or "casts a lot," as it's known in this practice—the outcome is believed to be divinely influenced. But can the runes allow us to connect with people who have passed on?

"We know for an absolute fact that the ancient Germanic runemasters thought that the runes were descended from the gods," Thorsson said. "In stanza 80 of the Eddic poem 'Havamal,' it is said of them literally that they are *reginkunnigar*—of divine descent. This same word is used to describe the runes on the sixth-century stone of Noleby. This and other mythic and historical evidence points to the fact that the runes are a gift from the gods, and more specifically from the god Odin.

"Obviously the runes are symbols for communication— communication between gods and men, men and the universe, and between human beings over time and space. The great and numerous runestones of Scandinavia are important parts of the communication between the living and the dead. The living memorialize, and hence immortalize, the dead. The living help the souls of the dead by means of the runic inscriptions on the stones.

"The Germanic tradition is full of practices for contacting the dead—especially dead ancestors. Ultimately, after all, the gods are such ancestors, although they are not generally conceived of as dead human beings. The runes can be used in this process."

Thorsson quoted the 157th stanza of the "Havamal":

That twelfth (Rune) I know,
if up on a tree I see
a hanged corpse swinging:
then I carve
and color the runes,
so that the man walks
and speaks with me.

Thorsson stated how many other regional folk tales, such as those from Iceland, also speak of interactions between the living and the dead.

"What do you think draws people to runes?" I asked.

"The Runes constitute what I call 'deep mysteries.' Only certain people are ever drawn to 'deep' mysteries. For the most part, people are drawn to conventional mysteries. Conventional mysteries are those which have an expected appearance in the popular mind-set. This is why things clothed in the appearances of popular symbolism (from Christianity to Hinduism) generally draw greater interest than do things belonging to deep structures. Those who are drawn to runes are drawn by the innate and authentic symbolic quality that they possess. The runes, and Germanic mythology, are *our own* deep symbols. Those who have tapped this deep reservoir within themselves have opened themselves to this deep source of wisdom. In short, those who are truly drawn to the runes are drawn by a profound sense of mysterious awe and authenticity."

There are a wide variety of ways to work with runes. I wanted to cover a few of the more simple methods. As with all of the subjects covered in this book, we're only touching the spirit world through each method and device covered. To explore deeper will require further study. One of the easiest ways to consult the runes is to ask a question that can be answered with a yes or no. *Is today a good day to ask my boss for a raise?* you might ask. Reach into your sack and pull out a single rune. If the symbol is face-up, the answer is "yes"; if it is face-down (sometimes called "inverted"), the answer is "no."

One might ask if a coin toss can achieve the same results with regard to a yes/no reading. The answer is yes...and no.

Statistically speaking, the coin will give you the same 50/50 chance at an objective and random yes or no answer to your question. However, to work with runes requires a deeper spirituality and belief. Experienced runecasters don't approach the runes with trivial questions. They take their craft seriously and are expecting solemn guidance from this system. To the experienced runecaster, there is nothing random, even with a one-rune reading—only the correct answers will come up every time. If you want to know whether to get pepperoni or meatballs on your pizza, flip a coin. If you want to know if today is the right day to start a new career, go with runes.

Another way to experience a one-rune reading is to ask a question such as: *What do I need to know for today to be successful?* Tir (↑) is the rune of victory. If you draw this symbol, plan carefully, but act decisively. If Tir is reversed (face-up, but the symbol is upside-down), it can mean a failure in competition possibly due to your impatience—so put extra effort into being patient. If you draw Eihwaz (↓) in a one-draw reading, the message is to keep up your defenses; today may not be the day to attack an issue, rather, hold it off for another day. With Eihwaz, there is no reversed meaning because this is one of several runes that is identical when reversed.

One of the more complicated methods involves the casting of lots—ceremoniously tossing the runes in your bag and then studying the pattern they make when they come to rest. The area where the bulk of the runes fall has one meaning; how the runes are arranged has another. Some runecasters disregard any runes that are face-down and unreadable, because if that is how they fell, then they were not important to the reading. There are countless spreads and methods to this practice. It's most important to follow what works best for you.

For my first rune reading, I decided to do a three-rune spread. Runes are read from right to left, so in this spread, the first rune I pick is placed on the right and represents the overview of my situation; the second, in the center, is the challenge; and the third, on the left, signifies the course of action. The question I asked was: *What can runes teach us about spirit communication?* I took my bag full of runes to a spot on the floor in a quiet part of my house. Many runecasters recommend spreading your runes on a special sheet or blanket each time. I used a bandana I've had for many years. The first rune I drew was Isa (I), the second was Daeg (M), and the third was Mannaz (M) reversed.

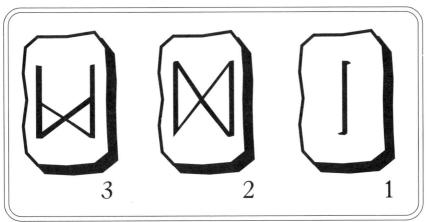

My first rune spread.

For meaning, I consulted Ralph Blum's *The Book of Runes*.

Overview: On Isa, Blum writes, "The winter of the spiritual life is upon you. You may find yourself entangled in a situation to whose implications you are, in effect, blind. You may feel powerless to do anything except submit, surrender, even sacrifice some long-cherished desire. Be patient, for this is the period of gestation that precedes a re-birth."

Isa means "ice" in modern English. I take this to mean there is no immediate gratification in regard to my question. In communicating with the spirit world, I am blind and powerless. I have only the testimony of others who have claimed to connect, though I myself have yet to make that profound contact. But because I'm asking the question and exploring the topic, the last sentence hints that a discovery is possible.

Challenge: On Daeg, Blum says, "[Drawing Daeg] often signals a major shift or breakthrough in the process of self-change, a complete transformation in attitude, a 180-degree turn. For some, the transition is so radical that they are no longer able to live the ordinary life in the ordinary way."

Daeg means "day" in modern English. The challenge in regard to my question may be to forget what I know or think I know of spirit communication. If I can change my perspective, the answer may be just ahead. This rune can mark the breaking dawn of this new day of spiritual enlightenment.

Action: On Mannaz reversed, Blum wrote, "If you feel blocked, Mannaz urges you to begin by being clear with yourself. Do not turn to others now, but look inside, in silence, for the enemy of your progress. No matter what area of your life is in disarray, stop and consider: You will recognize the outer enemy as but a reflection of what you have not, until now, been able or willing to recognize as coming from within."

Mannaz means "man" or "the self" in modern English. This rune sums up my own personal feelings on the very nature of spirituality: Although others can offer advice and insight, each of us is ultimately responsible for our own spirituality. It's a problem that each of us has to reach our own conclusions on. This implies that for spirit communication through the runes, I need to look within, which makes complete sense considering my runes are just pieces of clay. They are incapable of spirit communication—communication will need to come through me.

The more I studied the shapes and symbols contained within the runes, the more I began to spot them all around me and remember them from my own past. For example, I went to enough Grateful Dead concerts to know the rune Eolh (ᛉ) reversed and contained within a circle is the peace symbol. Some runes look very similar to some of our modern English letters, like Raidho (ᚱ) for "R," Wunjo (ᚹ) for "P," or Gifu (ᚷ)

for "X." Still others can be spotted on traffic signs, such as those marking a sharp curve like Kenaz (<). In Germany, there is an architecture style called *Fachwerk*, which is similar to the English Tudor or half-timbered styles. As the timbers intersect at various angles around the facades, you can clearly see several runes. To followers of this path, Odin speaks to us everywhere.

Runes are about self-study, but for those who are most serious, there are organizations to contact. In 1980, the Rune Gild (*www.runegild.org*) was founded by Edred Thorsson, with a mission to assist in the personal development of its members and to renew the tradition of the ancient Germanic and Indo-European cultures. Today, Thorsson serves as its *Yrmin-Drighten* (Grandmaster). He told me that, as of 2005, the Gild has locations in North America, Europe, and Australia and has about 500 members. The Gild is selective—they only accept 120 learners in North America at any one time.

"Given your 30 years of study in runes," I asked Edred Thorsson, "what changes have you seen to the practice?"

"Well, of course, the runes have not changed," he said. "They are eternal principles. They were understood in one way by our ancestors, and in a different way by us today, but the principles which they embody have not changed. Neither have runecasters changed—not as a group. Individuals change, but groups will always be made up of a hierarchy of individuals—those who are just learning the craft, those who are well on their way to mastery, and those who have become Masters and who have taken on the responsibility to teach. Over the past 30 years, we have seen a development of this system, but there is much more to be done in the future than has been done up to now. Since the writing of *Runecaster's Handbook: At the Well of Wyrd* in the late 1980s, new methods of runecasting have been rediscovered, which make use of the Younger Futhark of 16 runes."

There are deep mysteries in any esoteric field of study. For those who undertake the runes, the journey to resolve those mysteries is never-ending. The quest itself is what makes us grow. The desire to learn and then to learn more is where we begin to connect with the spiritual. Runes are a powerful tool for this study because though the symbols provide some answers, they also provide more questions. After all, what good would an oracle be if it gave you *all* of the answers and you never had to think for yourself?

The Futhark Runes

Fehu.   Modern English equivalent: F.

Uruz.   Modern English equivalent: U.

Thurisaz.   Modern English equivalent: Th.

Ansuz.   Modern English equivalent: A.

Raidho.   Modern English equivalent: R.

Kenaz.   Modern English equivalent: K.

Gifu.   Modern English equivalent: G.

Wunjo.   Modern English equivalent: W.

Hagall.   Modern English equivalent: H.

Nied.   Modern English equivalent: N.

Isa.   Modern English equivalent: I.

Jera.   Modern English equivalent: J.

Eihwaz.   Modern English equivalent: Ei.

Perdhro.   Modern English equivalent: P.

Eolh.   Modern English equivalent: Z.

Sigel.   Modern English equivalent: S.

Tir.   Modern English equivalent: T.

Beorc.   Modern English equivalent: B.

Ehwaz.   Modern English equivalent: E .

Mannaz.   Modern English equivalent: M.

Lagaz.   Modern English equivalent: L.

Ing.   Modern English equivalent: Ng.

Othel.   Modern English equivalent: O.

Daeg.   Modern English equivalent: D.

 Odin or Wyrd. This is a modern addition to the Futhark system; the blank symbol represents the unknowable. Some systems name the blank "Odin," after the god; others name it "Wyrd" ("weird" in modern English) after the collective term for the Norse sisters: Urdhr (past), Verthandi (present), and Skuld (future). They represent all knowledge.

"The mirror started to go smoky and blurry. Then it started to get backlit red, and I saw rows of silhouettes of people—just heads and shoulders, but they were rows deep....I'm sitting there trying to relax and trying to get into it, and something flew out of the bottom of the mirror and swooped straight at my head. It was so real that I had to jump out of the way."

8 Mirror Gazing

Reflections offer a different view of things—a backward and oftentimes flattened image, to be precise—but reflections have always intrigued us. Mirrors are everywhere; they're in our bathrooms, all over our cars, mounted on walls, and packed in women's purses. Finely polished mirrors power telescopes, from the cheapest toy version to the Hubble space telescope. There is much in folklore about covering mirrors in the house where someone dies. One superstition says the mirror can capture the dead person's soul. Another says that if a person sees his reflection anywhere in a room where someone has recently died, he will soon die, himself. Mirrors offer us a look at ourselves, can provide glimpses of faraway stars and planets, and sometimes find themselves central to superstitions surrounding death.

But can they offer us a view of other dimensions? Can we see the ethereal if we stare long enough and in just the right way?

Many say we can—if you know where and how to look. The concept of a mirror predates glass, even predates metallurgy. The first time man looked into a still pond and saw himself stare back, he considered it magic. He thought he was seeing his spirit gazing at him.

To see our reflection on demand, we needed a portable, reflective surface. Copper was the metal that served as the cornerstone for a more modern civilization. It was shiny and malleable, but on its own, it wasn't strong enough to be made into tools. Around 3900 B.C.E., Egyptians discovered that, by melting and combining copper with other metals such as tin, they could create bronze—a much sturdier metal—the first alloy. This marked the birth of the Bronze Age, an age where tools, art, and weapons rose to new levels of craftsmanship, strength, and technology.

As metallurgists improved their techniques and tools, metals took on any shape and shine their creator sought. Finely polished metals offered reflections to those who peered in to their depths. Some of the earliest mirrors were simply flat discs of polished copper, gold, and other metals.

Reflective surfaces and mirrors have been considered sacred for many centuries. The ancient Greeks were mesmerized by the reflections staring back through kettles, bowls, and cups. Some claimed to see visions in these objects. The people who saw these visions and places where they occured rose to oracle status and were consulted by kings and peasants alike. There were many oracles of ancient Greece—though the Oracle at Delphi was arguably the most famous.

The Oracle at Delphi was located in the Temple of Apollo at the top of Mount Parnassus in central Greece. Inside, the oracle stood waiting to offer prophecy in exchange for gold. This female seer was called Pythia. Many different women served as Pythia from roughly 1400 B.C.E. until 381 C.E., when Rome became a Christian empire and banned the practice of consulting oracles. Where Pythia got her visions from has been the cause of much debate. Many claim that gasses rose from beneath the temple caused by tectonic plates rubbing against each other beneath the ground and super-heating the rocks and minerals, allowing noxious vapors to make their way through cracks and fissures until it reached the surface and caused hallucinations. The gas may well have been rising through the ground, but ancient art and accounts of the Oracle at Delphi lead us to believe that Pythia may also have been getting vision from an optical depth.

The Oracle at Delphi was used for fortune telling and advice—anything from when to plant the harvest to when to attack a foe was speculated upon by the oracle. But there were other oracles around Greece—oracles of the dead—places where spirit contact was made through staring into polished cauldrons, bowls, and cups inside of dark caves and temples.

Ancient oracles appear in other traditions as well. The Jewish tradition has a similar story of their oracle.

Rabbi Gershon Winkler is a renowned Jewish scholar whose work encompasses Jewish folklore, theology, and the shamanic roots of the faith. The 56-year-old was born in Denmark, the son and grandson of a rabbi. He left Jewish Orthodoxy behind to explore a more free-spirited theology strongly tied to nature. I spoke to Rabbi Winkler from his home in the tiny village of Cuba, New Mexico. This was my second time speaking with Winkler. He's actually a very funny guy who has an easy-going way about him. His way of explaining different aspects of the Jewish faith is the most easily understood that I've ever found. He's also the author of more than a dozen books on Judaism, including *Kabbalah 365: Daily Fruit from the Tree of Life*.

"The Talmud tells us that there were 12 stones sewn into the priestly breastplate in ancient times," Winkler said. "If they [the leadership] didn't know an answer to a national question, like What should we do? Should we go to war? Should we do this? Do we do that? And if the elders couldn't answer the question, then they would come to the high priest. The priest would gaze on the stones with the question that was brought to him, and the stones would light up and give him the answer. We call the oracle the *Urim V'tumim*, which means 'illuminators and clarifiers.' To this day, we have no clue what that oracle was exactly. Some say in the Talmud that it was not a thing of this world. But whatever it was, it was embedded inside the breastplate that carried the stones."

"Is there any trace of that oracle today?" I asked.

"Not that we know of," Winkler said. "All of that stuff disappeared with the destruction of the first temple. The spiritual stuff like the Ark of the Covenant—which is now in a warehouse in Washington D.C."

"The Ark is in Washington D.C.?"

"Yes, didn't you see that movie, *Raiders of the Lost Ark*?"

Rabbi Winkler had a laugh at my expense.

"The Ark of the Covenant—that magic box that we carried—and the staff of Moses, which was inside that ark along with the tablets, the oracle, and the breastplate, all disappeared. We have no idea where it went. The Babylonians did not get a hold of it, because according to the Talmud, the ancient rabbis either sent it away to another country, and they surmised it was the land of Kush, which is Ethiopia. Or, another theory in the Talmud is that it was buried by the priests in one of the millions of catacombs underneath the Temple Mount area that they're still digging up today. A third theory is a wild one—that a great fire came down from the sky and just consumed all of those important pieces. So since 2,500 years ago, we have not had the oracle and we have not had the Arc. So all of our magical stuff has been done mostly through spirits and rituals."

During the First Council of Constantinople in 381 C.E., the Catholic Church began defining its dogmas and practices. Consulting oracles was out, because divination was deemed against scripture. By the fourth century, the Catholic Church had an official anathema on mirror gazing—they did not want their followers getting messages or visions from anything other than lore sanctioned by the Church. I find it interesting that, throughout the centuries, the Catholic Church has acknowledged some supernatural events happening to common folks, such as the three young children to whom Mary, the mother of Jesus, gave future prophecy during the miracle at Fatima, Portugal. I don't see why mirror gazing couldn't be used to explore one's own religion. The results are profound, and if taken in the context of one's belief system, I would imagine faith would be cemented and not shaken.

Dr. Raymond Moody, M.D., best-selling author of *Life After Life*, among several other books dealing with near-death experiences and the afterlife, has been intrigued with the ancient Greek oracles since his college days at the University of Virginia when he earned his Ph.D. in philosophy. "It's a subject I've been fascinated with from the very beginning, because the oracles of the dead have an important role in the foundation of Western philosophy," Moody said, when I spoke to him from his home in eastern Alabama.

Moody has a unique blend of science and philosophy in his background. Also being a medical doctor, he understands the physiology as well as the mentality of people—especially concerning the subject of death, dying, and grief. This conversation was the second time I had the pleasure of interviewing Dr. Moody. He speaks with fondness and fascination when we discuss issues of viewing the spirit world and the question of life after death. "I don't have any idea whether there's life after death or not," Moody said. "It really seems to me that the question of life after death is not yet ripe for scientific inquiry because it's not formulatable in a way that fits into the scientific method. But I also think it's *the* most important question. If you think of the big questions of existence, this is the biggie."

Many are trying to apply science to this very question. I'm just as guilty from within these very pages. For my own spiritual quest, I feel that if I can just capture enough evidence through logical means, then the equation will add up to the notion of an afterlife. Life after death is a hypothesis that many of us share, but for now, anyway, the proof has to come on the individual level. A more realistic pursuit is one where we each seek enough evidence to satisfy our own intellects on the subject. Certainly the sense of sight offers us some of the most compelling evidence. We believe our own eyes, right? And there's another well-known saying: the mirror doesn't lie. If the mirror shows an individual visions of lost loved ones, that may be all of the evidence needed to create proof for that person.

Back in the 1980s, Dr. Moody garnered interested in the concept of mirror gazing after picking up an old book called *Crystal Gazing*, published in 1905, at a used bookstore. The idea made him think of the ancient Greeks and their oracles of the dead:

> I found out in the 1980s that a Greek classical archaeologist named Sotirios Dakaris had gone to the place that Herodotus, Homer, Pausanias, Strabo, and many others describe where this most

famous oracle was—directly below modern-day Albania—and they dug it up. In their excavation, in the central apparition hallway, they found a big, bronze cauldron. I surmised that what they were doing was inducing altered states of consciousness by gazing into mirrors or clear bodies of water, or other reflective surfaces. You don't look at the reflections; you just gaze into the depth.

The Greeks were the first that we know of to follow this practice of seeing visions, but Moody believes it's probable that the idea of gazing into a clear optical depth goes even further back. The practice has never really gone away since the days of ancient Greece, and it crosses many geographic borders and religious backgrounds. "My own ancestors, the Cherokee, did it in clear ponds," Moody said. "Aztec shaman had quartz crystals they held in their hand, and they also used polished obsidian mirrors." People in the Middle East still polish silver bowls and peer into them, seeking visions. Some Hindus have been known to rub oil on their thumbnail to seek visions in the optical depth created.

A typical crystal ball available at many metaphysical shops. Photo by Jeff Belanger.

Legends and lore also come into play here. For centuries, some believed certain weaponry, such as swords, had spirits attached to them—spirits you could see when you gazed into the finely polished blade. The tale of Aladdin and his lamp may very well have been inspired by the real-life practice of polishing metal objects, such as lamps, to gaze in and see spirits—perhaps those spirits became his "genie" in the story. Crystal balls can also be used. "Anything that will give you a clear optical depth will provoke these visions," Moody said.

Dr. Moody took what he knew of mirror gazing and developed a mechanism to try and make these visions accessible to everyone. He devised a psychomanteum chamber.

The psychomanteum chamber is a small, dark room, approximately 10 feet × 10 feet—with a 4-foot × 3 1/2-foot mirror on one wall and black material all around. A cushioned chair with the legs cut off and slightly reclined sits facing the mirror from 3 feet away, and an electric light with a 15-watt bulb is plugged in behind the chair, which offers just enough light to illuminate the room so one can see the mirror. The reason a light bulb is used and not a candle is because the bulb offers steady light that won't flicker and cause moving shadows the way a candle would, if there were any disturbance or air movement in the little room. The user of the chamber sits in the chair and looks up into the mirror—it's important that the person and the mirror be positioned so the user can't see any part of his own reflection—just a clear, dark, optical depth.

The idea may seem rather gothic and ceremonial, but the reasoning is actually quite simple. "The reason I use the chamber with the black material and everything is because that enhances the likelihood that somebody will see something on the first attempt, just by the sensory deprivation," Moody said. "But you don't really need a chamber; you can do the same things with a handheld mirror."

"Have you ever experienced spirit contact through mirror gazing?" I asked.

"Definitely, in the sense that I've seen my grandmother," he said. "Now, was that spirit contact or not? What I can't make up in my mind is: Is this 'real' or is it not? I don't think that's a rational determinable question. But yes, I've had the experience. It's interesting to me that far and away the greatest number of people that I take through [the psychomanteum chamber] do have an experience and they absolutely do interpret it to be a reality. And I can understand how they do, because I saw my grandmother with great vividness and clarity. But still, just the way my mental process works, I'm not ready to draw an inference that I really did see my grandmother."

My friend Jim DeCaro had the opportunity to visit Dr. Moody and go through the psychomanteum chamber. DeCaro explained how Moody prepares people for the chamber by talking them through the possibilities and their expectations. "He's trying to gauge if something were to show up how you would handle it," DeCaro said. "He's concerned with seeing what kind of mind frame people are in." Moody explores each user's expectations and leads them through a period of relaxation and focusing before going in. If a user of the chamber were looking to contact someone specific on the other side, he or she may focus on photographs or mementos of that person before going in.

DeCaro wasn't looking to make contact with anyone specific. He was open to whatever this experience would bring. "What was your frame of mind when you first sat down in this chamber?" I asked.

"I wanted to try and slip into a passive state," DeCaro said. "It's a little difficult at first, and it takes a little bit of time, because you have to get over that anxiousness. That's the difficult part of it—every second you're saying, 'Am I going to see something? Am I going to see something?' At that point, you're too nervous for it to work."

"Did the psychomanteum chamber work for you?"

"Two things happened to me. First, the mirror started to go smoky and blurry. Then it started to get backlit red, and I saw rows of silhouettes of people—just heads and shoulders, but they were rows deep. Then, on my second trip into the chamber, something flew out of the mirror and came straight at my head. I'm sitting there trying to relax and trying to get into it, and something flew out of the bottom of the mirror and swooped straight at my head. It was so real that I had to jump out of the way."

"Was that the end of the experience?" I asked. "Did you try again after that?"

"I stayed there and tried to get back into it, but that was pretty much it. It was actually a very cool experience."

In his book, *The Psychic in You*, psychic Jeffrey Wands describes his experience in Dr. Moody's psychomanteum chamber. After being prepped by Moody, Wands sat in the chair and tried to let go and relax. He writes that he felt as though he was moving toward the mirror—he described it as more of a cerebral movement as opposed to a physical movement. He described a tunnel in front of him with a diamond-shaped light at the end that grew larger as he moved forward. In the book, Wands writes, "people started to appear...without faces. Still, I recognized most of them. Neighbors, kids who had died when I was young, old people, aunts, and uncles. They filed by me on both sides, touching me, an army of the dead, but an army I was not afraid of, nor were they afraid of me."

The William James Center for Consciousness Studies Institute of Transpersonal Psychology in Palo Alta, California, published a study in 2002 called "Psychomanteum Research: Experiences and Effects on Bereavement." The study was published in *Omega: Journal of Death and Dying* and reported on the Institute's findings about people who went through a psychomanteum chamber based on Dr. Moody's design.

The study, conducted by Arthur Hastings et al, brought 27 participants through a series of interviews, a session within the chamber, and a post-experience review. The participants were asked to focus on a specific deceased person whom they wished to contact. The study made no claim (or denial) that there would be actual spirit communication. Out of 27 people (19 women and eight men), 17 claimed to have received some kind of results from within the chamber. The experiences ranged from memories or thoughts of the person they were focusing on, to sensing the deceased person's personality and actually having a dialogue with that person/spirit.

I asked Moody if he still uses the psychomanteum chamber today. "No I don't," he said. "I still mirror gaze regularly, but I do it now mostly for creativity, which is another good use of it. It helps get ideas."

"How so?"

"You'll just formulate yourself a question, and then you gaze into the mirror or your crystal ball or whatever and you start seeing visions. They help you out in your creative process."

There is a term called "mirror scrying" that I had heard of from some of my Witch friends. At first pass, the concept sounds very similar to mirror gazing—and it is, but the intent is where mirror gazing and scrying separate. Scrying is using mirrors or clear optical depths for divination—or trying to foresee future events. Allegedly, famed seer Nostradamus was scrying in a bowl of water when he saw his visions of the future. This concept has other esoteric applications, but my main interest lies in the spirit communication aspect of it.

From talking with Dr. Moody, I was beginning to understand that mirror gazing is about visually exploring your subconscious mind. Whether those visions are merely a hallucination, or "waking dream," or an actual view of an ethereal plane is the debate. On one side of the argument, who cares? The ends—which are profound visions—may not necessitate comprehending the means. On the other hand, how does it work?

"Exactly. And I'm one of those who cares," Moody said. "I would like to know, although I don't think I'm going to be able to find out. Our logic doesn't allow passing from that experience, no matter how profound and lasting it may be, to any sort of rational conclusion about it. That's a facet of the aspect of our logic."

Asking anyone to believe "miracle" testimony, or supernatural hearsay, is asking a lot. This is the leap of faith that most world religions depend on for survival. If people don't believe hearsay testimony of supernatural miracles, then the foundation of the religion falls to pieces. Yet, we all lack the basic understanding of what the supernatural is. We can't comprehend it because we don't even have the words in our vocabulary to describe these things—just general terms such as: *supernatural, paranormal, ghost, spirit, specter,* and so on. We lack the words to truly describe the emotions that swell inside of us during one of these encounters. My own faith in the supernatural is based on the aftermath the experience has left. When I speak to someone who has truly had an encounter, I can see the profound nature of the encounter—it has changed him forever—maybe in a subtle way, or maybe in a big, life-altering way. To understand the experience, we must go through it ourselves. We must try to look at the other side. Does the mirror hold the power for any of us to look into the spirit world?

For my own mirror gazing experiments, I decided to build my own device: a black mirror. On the advice of a Witch friend, I followed a rather simple plan: I found an old framed picture in my basement. (It was a rather tacky, earth-toned sketch of a potted topiary and was matted in hunter green—one of those cheap pictures one buys with one's wife when one is trying to fill blank wall space in one's first apartment.) I went to the local arts and crafts store and spent about $3.50 on a tube of black paint, a piece of black poster board, and a sponge-brush.

I dismantled the picture frame until I had just the glass and the frame.

My dismantled picture frame. Photo by Jeff Belanger.

Next, I thoroughly cleaned the glass using a specific magic solution suggested to me by my Witch friend (Windex). I used the sponge-brush to paint the black paint on one side of the glass. I then used a magic drying device to accelerate the process (my wife's hairdryer). I could see from the many specks of white showing through that this would take multiple coats of paint. It took three before I had the glass fully covered.

I cut the poster board to the same size as the glass and then reassembled the frame, first putting in the glass (with the shiny, unpainted surface facing out), next the black poster board, and finally the cardboard padding so I could tap in the metal clips to hold it all together. I now had my black mirror.

My completed black mirror. Photo by Jeff Belanger.

Though I'd heard of black mirrors before, I'd never actually seen one, much less made one. Gazing into the dark depth of the mirror, I was definitely intrigued.

For my gazing exercise, I chose a quiet, uncluttered part of my house. In my first attempt, I laid the black mirror on the floor facing up. I sat back comfortably against a wall and stared at the black mirror. I'd positioned myself so I could not see my reflection, but I could see the line where the ceiling met the wall, and I could see the edge of the door molding that ran up to the ceiling. I could also see the edge of a lighting fixture.

I took a deep breath and tried to focus on the mirror. At first I stared at the lighting fixture, and as I stared, the fixture started to fade to black. Soon everything in the mirror became a blurry black. I couldn't hold this gaze very long because my eyes' natural reflex was to refocus. With a blink, everything came back into normal focus again. I stared at another point, the edge of where the ceiling met the wall, and within 20 seconds or so, I also experienced the fade to black. I tried staring at the ceiling in general—not at any specific point— but I couldn't reproduce the blackout effect.

The entire exercise lasted about 20 minutes. At one point, I did see what looked like a small cloud just off-center of the black mirror—it looked almost like the satellite view of a hurricane or some other fat vortex. The color was dark gray, so it mostly blended in with the background. I can't swear this wasn't a byproduct of my eyes going in and out of focus, but it was something I saw.

For my next attempt, I was going to use a regular mirror. In my basement I had a large, 2-foot by 3-foot plate-glass mirror that I took out of my bathroom when I remodeled it last year. For this experiment, I wanted to try and create something closer to the psychomanteum chamber. I set my mirror up in my upstairs hallway and closed all of the doors. I used a very low-wattage electric candle for light and placed it behind me. I used pillows and a dark sleeping bag to place against a bench I moved out into the hall so it would support my back. I laid down and stared directly into the mirror at the white ceiling above.

After about five minutes, I noticed my blurry vision returning, like in my first attempt with the dark mirror, but this time my eyes were not struggling to go back in focus. I found myself focusing near the top of the mirror. My breathing was slow, steady, and rhythmic. Along the top edge of the mirror, I observed what looked like very faint static—like a channel on your television that doesn't come in. The static was only at the top edge, hardly noticeable except for a few dark and light specks that flitted here and there. At this point I actually became a little nervous. I found myself internally asking questions such as, "What if I see a face? Am I ready for that?" I felt my heart rate increase slightly. I calmed down again and continued to stare.

I did see two things. I know this sounds strange, but I saw a fly—an ordinary housefly, but from my perspective it was the size of a football. It was mostly transparent, not animated at all, and it faded after one to two seconds, but it was very clearly a fly. I don't think I saw it in the mirror because I've had this kind of thing happen before—usually after waking up suddenly from a dream and still seeing an image from my dream in my bedroom for a second or two, though I'm awake and my eyes are open and I recognize my surroundings. The medical community refers to this as a "hypnopompic hallucination"—basically a waking dream. Why I saw a fly, I have no idea; it was during a rather cold November week in Massachusetts, and there hadn't been any flies around in several weeks.

The second "vision" I saw was an intricate mask—almost like an African tribal mask with stark angled lines on the cheeks, a pronounced nose, and lines along the forehead. This appeared in the same manner, size, and semitranslucent way the fly appeared. I don't have an explanation for this image either. I've seen these types of masks before, but I can't say I'd been thinking about them lately.

My own experiences with mirror gazing were definitely intriguing, and now that I'm safely away from the mirror and writing this, I don't think I am ready for anything more than what I saw. Had a vivid image of a dead relative appeared before me, I know I would have been scared. I didn't expect to see anything, but when the static started, the thought crossed my mind that it was possible I would see something. That fear is what broke my relaxed state.

During my session, I know my eyes were focusing, blurring, and even straining at times. For a better understanding of what my eyes were going through, I placed a call back to ophthalmologist Dr. Lawrence K. Fox. I explained to him what I had gone through in front of both the black and regular mirrors.

"When you're looking at an object, both eyes are pointed toward that object and focused," he said. "You know those 3-D books that were so popular a few years ago?"

"Sure, the ones where you stare at some colorful, chaotic design and then suddenly you see something recognizable three-dimensionally in the page," I said.

"Exactly. With those 3-D books, you let your eyes relax so that they're going to focus further away than the plane of the book. In other words, when you're looking at a certain distance behind the book, your brain is going to interpret the two dissimilar images from the eyes as stereo."

With the 3-D books, your eyes still see the 2-D image on the page in front of you, but they also see the imaginary point beyond the image. Your brain then falsely interprets and combines the two different pieces of information coming in. The flat picture on the book and the point beyond the image, when blended, cause a three-dimensional picture to emerge.

"The same is true with mirror gazing," Fox said. "The brain is receiving two different images—it's not looking at one object, and weird things can start to happen."

The mirror is also a two-dimensional image. And the point of mirror gazing is to look beyond that image, just as with those 3-D books, so our brain gets confused. "What kinds of weird things?" I asked.

"The brain can sometimes fill in things," he said. "It can cause black rings around the outside [of your field of vision], for example. You have to remember that the brain is processing all of this. The eyes aren't making anything happen—they just simply report data to the optic nerve, and the optic nerve takes it to the brain, and that's where vision is processed."

Whether this focusing or lack thereof is what causes simple hallucinations or bona fide supernatural visions is up to the person who has the experience. Even if one wants to take the most skeptical and pragmatic approach to mirror gazing and say we're simply seeing images from our subconscious, that's still an experience worth having.

The nature of hallucinations is important to understand. We all have them every day of our lives—each time we dream it's a hallucination. As I mentioned earlier, we can also have hypnopompic hallucinations (those visions that occur just as we wake up) or hypnagogic hallucinations (those visions that occur just as we fall asleep), though both are rare. The only times I've experienced hypnopompic hallucinations are when waking from a dream when my morning clock radio alarm goes off. I may be dreaming about seeing a mountain, then the alarm suddenly wakes me. I open my eyes and still see the mountain, though I'm also very conscious of seeing my bedroom. Within a second or two, the dream vision fades and I see only my room.

It's very difficult for psychiatrists or even neuroscientists to comment on hallucinations in general, because of the myriad of potential causes. A person may be taking narcotics or suffering from schizophrenia, but there are perfectly healthy people who have what they believe to be visions within a spiritual context such as mirror gazing.

Though we may not fully understand why or how these visions are happening, one hypothesis is that hallucinations are triggered by an overactivity of dopamine in the area of the brain that processes perception, emotions, and thought. The result of this chemical reaction can be disturbances in thought-processing, memory, or emotions, as well as hallucinations and/or delusions.

When people are brought to the hospital because of an overdose of an hallucinogenic drug such as LSD or PCP, their pupils are often extremely dilated because the eyes are trying to take in the sensory overload that is perceived to be occurring outside of the body. The visions for these people are clearly real, because their eyes react physiologically.

In a normal, healthy person who is not taking narcotics, these mirror or crystal gazing visions (or hallucinations and/or delusions, depending on your skepticism) are perceived as a very real, profound, and spiritual event.

The mirror *doesn't* lie. And if our eyes are the windows to our souls, then mirror gazing is an accessible method to look within. Visions are the objective of this practice. To experience them, we need to conquer our fear of what we might see, but this is easier said than done. Fredrich Nietzsche once wrote, "If you gaze for long into an abyss, the abyss gazes also into you." Before we sit before the mirror, we need to be prepared for a revelation, whether it's from the furthest depths of our mind or from the spirit world.

"We watched the stone [pendulum] actually move in an X-shape. **Everybody could see it**, not just me. I felt the energy—it was there.... I could feel somebody lifting up the weight of it, and the [EMF] meter was blaring under the stone."

Dowsing

At noon, I walked out to my mailbox to retrieve my daily dose of bills, junk mail, and sweepstakes promises, but today there was something else in there as well. I pulled out a small, brown envelope that contained a pair of "Original Bob Slack L-rods" that I had bought online for $12. I tore open the package. The thin, copper tube handles are 4 inches long, and the rods that come out of the handles at a 90-degree angle extend for 8 inches and freely swing 360 degrees—an important feature if these "pointers" are going to be easily moved by subtle energies.

Having been a dowser for almost two minutes now, I took them for an immediate test-drive in my backyard. I walked at a slow pace on a chilly, overcast autumn day in the early afternoon. Every few steps, I hesitated a bit as the copper rods began to sway to one side, then cross each other. I wasn't looking for spirits per se, but I was open to the idea of some outside force affecting the rods in my hands. I stopped and let the rods settle, then stepped again. I walked from one side of the yard to the other, in a large oval. The rods continued to swing and cross, and the notion that something otherworldly was moving them made me look around once or twice. Is it a ghost? Am I over water? Are any of my neighbors looking? At this stage in my dowsing research, I attributed the rods' movement mainly to gravity and centrifugal force caused by my own steps.

I realized I had no idea what I was doing and had better learn a few things before trying this again.

I'd first heard about dowsing as a child. One of my friends had a grandfather who could dowse for water using a forked stick. He used to work for the water company and was so matter-of-fact about his "gift" that I didn't get the impression that this was any gift at all. To this old-timer, dowsing was a simple fact—you walk around with a forked stick and you'll feel the stick pull down when you're over water. He claimed to have found many underground water pipes when he and his crew had to make repairs and replacements, wells, and any other water source that needed finding. To this man, it was a matter of paying attention—nothing supernatural at all.

Once I started researching the history of dowsing, I learned that people have found a lot more than just water. The technique also has been used to find metals, lost objects, people, animals, buried treasure, precious gems, even oil. In the early 1940s, a farmer in West Edmond, Oklahoma, J.W. Young, used a goatskin-covered bottle hanging from a chain to dowse for oil on his property. The pendulum swung north to south when Young walked over oil. The farmer convinced wildcatter Ace Gutowski to drill where he dowsed, and in 1943, Gutowski struck one of the largest deposits of oil in Oklahoma history. And this wasn't the only oil deposit to be found by a dowser.

A practice also called "divining" and even "witching," these rods and the techniques for using them are certainly a part of divination. Even matter-of-fact water dowsers are using the rods to foresee something: Is there water underground? If so, how deep? How strong? And if dowsing for physical things such as water and metals isn't supernatural enough, many people today are also dowsing for ethereal energy and believe this practice can be used to communicate with spirits.

Some typical tools of this trade include:

L-rods: Also called angle rods, swing rods, or pointing tools. The form of L-rods can vary from solid pieces of metal, pieces of plastic, to even bent coat hangers.

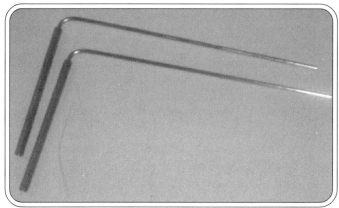

Photo by Jeff Belanger.

Y-rods: Also known as a forked stick or talking stick. These are shaped like a Y and can be made of metal, plastic, or a forked tree branch.

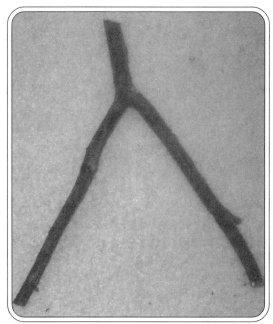

Photo by Jeff Belanger.

Pendulum: Simply a weighted object hanging from a string or chain.

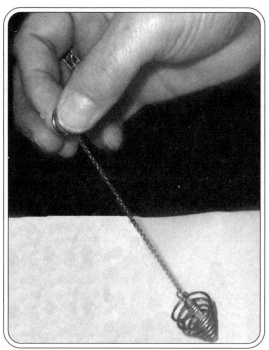

Photo by Jeff Belanger.

Expert dowsers will tell you that the most critical piece of the equation is you, the dowser. The power is in the person; the rods, sticks, and other implements simply act as the indicator needle on the supernatural compass around us all.

"Everyone is a dowser," said Ray Machell, provost for the American Society of Dowsers (ASD). The American Society of Dowsers (*www.dowsers.org*) was founded in 1961 in the small town of Danville, Vermont—just northwest of the state capital of Montpelier. The group's mission, as stated on their Website, is "to embrace those who seek to experience expanded consciousness through dowsing." Machell is a 67-year-old resident of Barre, Vermont, whose northern New England accent gives him away as a native. He's been dowsing since the mid-1990s and has taught more than 2,000 people how to do it. There's a surprisingly high concentration of dowsers in the New England area. To find out why, we need to go backward through history.

Dowsing's exact origins cannot be pinpointed, but we know there is evidence of dowsing from millennia ago, wherever there was civilization. "If you look back at the hieroglyphs of ancient Egypt, the bulk of what they were holding in their hands were dowsing tools," Machell said.

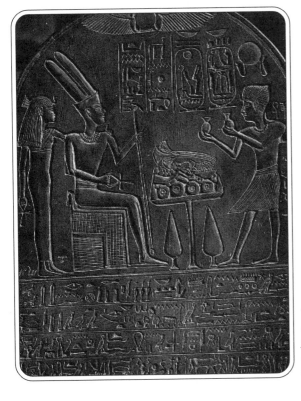

The ancient Egyptians used dowsing to find water and for spiritual purposes inside sacred sites. Photo courtesy of the Library of Congress.

Many scholars believe the first literary mention of dowsing can be found in the Bible. The dowser, in this account, is Moses:

> 5And the Lord said to Moses, "Pass on before the people, taking with you some of the elders of Israel; and take in your hand the rod with which you struck the Nile, and go. 6Behold, I

will stand before you there on the rock at Horeb; and you shall strike the rock, and water shall come out of it, that the people may drink." And Moses did so, in the sight of the elders of Israel. (Exodus 17:5–6)

According to Christopher Bird's book, *The Divining Hand*, the origin of the word "dowse" is actually uncertain, though the word made its first appearance in print in English philosopher John Locke's 1691 essay, "Some Considerations of the Consequences of the Lowering of Interest and the Raising the Value of Money." In his essay, Locke writes: "All the imaginable ways of increasing Money in any Country, are these two: Either to dig it in Mines of our own, or get it from our Neighbours. That Four per Cent. is not of the nature of the Deusing-rod, or Virgula Divina [water witching], able to discover Mines of Gold and Silver, I believe will easily be granted me." Locke is referring to finding precious metals by dowsing.

Bird believes Locke spelled the word "deusing" in an effort to phonetically spell a word he had known since childhood in Somersetshire, England.

History may not have an exact answer for the origin of the word, but English folklore does. According to the story, centuries ago a man with the surname "Dowse" helped the king find things through metaphysical means. The king dubbed the term *dowsing* in his honor. No matter the origin, the name has stuck.

In the 1600s, dowsers came from England to America to help locate water sources for new settlements. The dowsers referred to the practice as "divining"—a term that is still used today with some people—but the Massachusetts Puritans referred to the practice as "witching," giving it a dark undertone. By the late 1600s, talk of Witchcraft was spreading throughout northern Massachusetts. The Witch hunts reached a crescendo with the Salem Witch trials of 1692, and some dowsers or diviners found themselves facing the gallows for helping people find water. Many headed north to Vermont and northern New England and even Canada (where dowsers are called "questers") for refuge. But people never stopped dowsing.

During a 1960 Fall Foliage Festival in Danville, Vermont, several local dowsers got together and decided to display and teach dowsing at future festivals. The following year, they incorporated the American Society of Dowsers.

Ray Machell was introduced to the practice when a member of an amateur radio club he belonged to put a pendulum in his hands. "It took off like a propeller," he said. "I mean, it just went." He saw a flyer for dowsing classes offered by the ASD and soon joined the organization.

"What did you dowse for first?" I asked him.

"I did a lot of practicing once I discovered all of the great things you can do sitting in the living room at night with a pendulum and the L-rods," Machell said. "I experimented a lot with refining how to ask questions and doing a lot of reading."

I was beginning to understand that dowsing isn't just about finding water or minerals, or even sensing the supernatural. Here's my own oversimplified definition of dowsing: an ancient practice that uses tools to find something—*anything*, really.

The trick, I would learn, is knowing what questions to ask and how to focus your intent.

"If you take the rods in your hand, or your pendulum, or anything else," Machell said, "and you say, 'Does my car need gas?' you get a yes. Your car needs gas to run. Air is a gas; your car needs air to run. Of course your car needs gas. So you have to learn to ask very specific questions."

One question dowsers get asked a lot is, where's the water?

In many areas, if you're building a new home and there is no public water system to tap into, you'll need to drill for a well. According to Machell, if you call a well company to come drill your well, almost half of them will recommend you get a dowser to pick the spot to drill. Without a dowser, and assuming the well-drilling company doesn't have detailed information about the location of underground aquifers and veins, they're more or less wildcatting. Machell has dowsed close to 300 wells for people around Vermont since 2001.

Machell began dowsing for wells under the guidance of Paul Sevigny, a former president of the ASD who died in 2000. Sevigny had more than 7,000 wells to his credit. It's critical to have an experienced dowser around to verify a rookie's findings, because making a mistake on a well can be costly. "You read the books, you do everything else, and it works really great," Machell said. "But then to go out onto somebody's property and point to a spot on the ground and say, 'Okay, spend $5,000 of your money right on that spot right there,' that's pretty hairy the first few times."

I asked Machell how the process works when he goes to a location to dowse for a well. He explained how he uses one L-rod when he first gets out of his vehicle, to get a general direction of where to look for water. After doing this so many times, he's basically programmed his mind to look for water in an area that the drilling rig can fit and that's as convenient as possible to the house. Once he has a bearing, he uses an L-rod in each hand and follows them until they cross. When he has the spot, he asks a series of questions to determine the depth, quality, and force of the water. If the rods cross, the answer is yes; if they stay parallel, the answer is no. *Is the water less than 50 feet?* Machell may ask aloud. If the rods don't cross, he'll go to 60 feet, then 70, and so on. He uses the same technique to determine force. *Is it one gallon per minute of force? Two gallons?* When he's determined that the volume and depth are acceptable, he uses a pendulum to focus in to within an inch or so on where to dig.

"Everybody is a dowser, but a lot of people don't know it," Machell said. "I've probably been to about six different places where they called me and I take my rods and I go roaming around the property and I say, 'Boom, okay, here's the spot.' I look down and I see a red flag. And I'll say, 'Has there been a dowser here?' 'No.' And I'll say, 'What's this red flag?' They'll say the guy came in, looked around, and pointed over there, and said 'There is a good spot the truck will fit.' And the flag's dead on."

But what if you're not on the property? Can dowsing be done remotely? Map dowsing has been in use for almost as long as there have been maps. People used pendulums to try and determine where to dig for buried treasure, where to mine, or even where someone may have lost their wallet. "If you were building a house and you sent me a map up here, I will map dowse it with a pendulum and get exactly the same results as if I came down there," Machell said. "It makes no difference. What you're doing is you're tuning into what you are looking for. And it doesn't matter where it is—anywhere in the universe, it doesn't matter."

A large aerospace corporation in Queensland, Australia, contacted Machell because they had drilled six dry holes at $9,000 each while looking for water for their new facility. The company mailed him a map of the property. "I map dowsed it and gave them measurements; they drilled the hole and got their water," he says with a touch of pride in his voice.

Dowsing has been tested by science and remains unproven. One such person who has done a lot of dowser testing is James Randi—known by many as "The Amazing" Randi. Randi is a former stage magician who has performed at such notable venues as *The Tonight Show with Johnny Carson* and even at the White House. "I know how to fool people," he said to me from his office at the James Randi Educational Foundation (*www.randi.org*), also known as JREF, in Fort Lauderdale, Florida. "Most magicians do, but they do it mostly for purposes of entertainment. And I know how people fool themselves—and that's even more important."

Randi is a passionate skeptic. He started JREF in 1996, its mission: "To promote critical thinking by reaching out to the public and media with reliable information about paranormal and supernatural ideas so widespread in our society today." His organization offers a $1 million prize to anyone who can show paranormal, supernatural, or occult power under observed conditions. This includes people who claim they can dowse for objects.

"How many dowsers have you tested over the years?" I asked Randi.

James Randi. Photo courtesy of the James Randi Educational Foundation.

"Hundreds," he said. "It's pretty hard to keep track, because a great number of the tests are aborted when they find out they can't do it. So you don't know whether to count those are not. Most of them are aborted halfway through when they see they're not succeeding because it's a double-blind test."

A double-blind test is one where neither the evaluator nor the subject knows what the controls of the experiment are. The point is to reduce error, self-deceptions, and biases of both the evaluator and the subject. A real-life example makes this concept more easily understood:

In March of 2002, the JREF tested the dowsing claims of a Mr. G. (I'm withholding his last name to protect his privacy.) Mr. G. claimed he was an expert at finding gold using a forked stick. He brought 17 objects he would try to find during the experiment: a gold nugget, a gold ring, some "Sacagawea" U.S. dollar coins, some quartz crystals, and a vial of water.

All of these items were placed in a small plastic bag. Mr. G. then wrapped a small piece of gold around the tip of his forked stick in order to tune it into gold. This is not an uncommon practice among dowsers—a water dowser may dip the tip of their instruments in water, for example.

Next, 10 coffee cups were numbered one through 10, and 10 cards were also numbered. At Mr. G.'s direction, the 10 cups were spread around the floor of a large room at the JREF facility right-side up so the inside of each mug was accessible.

The numbered cards were shuffled and then one was chosen at random. Each numbered card corresponded to the one of the mugs. For example, if card #6 was chosen, then the bag full of gold items was placed into mug #6—this was all under the supervision of Mr. G. Keep in mind that everyone in the room, including Mr. G. and James Randi, knew exactly where the gold was at this point. Mr. G. then dowsed to find the gold and was—not surprisingly—successful.

This part of the test was repeated 19 more times by selecting random cards, placing the gold package in a cup, and then Mr. G. dowsing to find the gold. Though this may seem a bit silly at first, the baseline test is done to give the dowser the opportunity to discover any problems with the process, such as interference from something else, and it also allows the subject to get used to nature of the test.

In the next phase, the process was repeated. Then both Mr. G. and James Randi left the room while independent testers selected a card at random and placed the gold package in the corresponding coffee cup. But this time, all of the mugs were upside-down, so unless you saw where the package was placed, you would have a one-in-10 chance at guessing the correct mug.

Mr. G. then went through with his dowsing stick, but this time he found the gold only one out of every 10 attempts. To date, no one has claimed the JREF's million dollars for dowsing or any other supernatural feat.

"Does anyone test themselves before they come to you?" I asked.

"They say they do, but then when you get to question them after they failed, they say, 'Well, I didn't do a double-blind because I knew it wasn't necessary to do,'" Randi said. "They can't do a proper test unless it is double-blinded with another agent in there who is able to blind it for them."

"Has anyone tried to cheat the dowsing test?"

"Only two," he said. "One in Australia and one in the UK. Otherwise they're quite honest, but they're self-deluded. The vast majority of them really believe they've got the power or they wouldn't be coming to me, because I don't think anyone is unaware of the fact that I'm pretty hard to fool."

For those who use dowsing, they simply know it works—even if it can't be proven under controlled conditions. Finding water, metals, minerals, and more with dowsing is certainly a form of divination. You're asking someone or something for guidance. Whether that someone or something is your higher self or a higher power is the enigma of the matter. If you're asking something spirit-based to guide your dowsing tools, then spirit communication not only seems plausible, but expected of dowsing.

Today, many paranormal investigators are beginning to make dowsing a standard part of their practice. Judging from the diverse group of items that people have dowsed for, it seems to me that intent is the most critical aspect of what you will find. By setting out with a singular intent, dowsers are convinced they'll find what they're looking for.

"Imagine yourself like a radio," said Joey Korn, founder of Dowsers.com, energy worker, and author of *Dowsing: A Path to Enlightenment.* "Setting your intent is like tuning the frequencies on the dial. When you're looking for an underground stream of water, you're going to the energy frequency of an underground stream. Your rods are literally like antennas. You tune in through the rods—really through your mind—and the rods show you when you find the right frequency."

I spoke to Korn from his home in Augusta, Georgia. Korn is 51 years old, and he and his wife, Jill, sell dowsing equipment and books and conduct lectures and seminars full-time. I bought my L-rods from his Website.

Korn first learned about dowsing as a child from watching old Westerns on TV, such as *The Real McCoys.* He watched Grandpa McCoy dowsing with a forked stick on the show and went outside to give it a try. "We had a willow tree in our backyard, and I cut off a branch, but it just never worked for me. I had accepted the myth that was propagated in these old movies and that a lot of people still believe—that you have to be born with the gift. Since I didn't get a reaction, I figured I wasn't born with the gift."

His second introduction to dowsing came in 1986 when his family's lake house was having septic problems. A septic tank

service came out to the property and spent two hours searching for the tank until they finally gave up. "Then I called a
government agency and a nice old man answered the phone
and said, 'I'll find that septic tank for you,'" Korn said. "He
came out and literally in two minutes he found the septic
tank with a pair of bent-up coat hangers. And I was sold. He
taught me to dowse, and he helped me to know that everybody
can dowse."

"So when you tried dowsing for yourself, were you just
looking for water?" I asked.

"Actually, when I first started, I was looking for the septic
tank."

"That's some dirty water."

He laughed. For Joey Korn, dowsing quickly became a very
spiritual venture. He was raised in Judaism and says he'll die
Jewish. When I asked him how dowsing fits into his belief
system, Korn feels that dowsing not only fits in with his faith,
it also helps prove its validity.

The Kabbalah is an ancient aspect of Jewish mysticism.
The study is considered by many to be an esoteric offshoot of
Judaism because of the magical, meditative, and mystical practices it teaches. In the Jewish faith, there is some debate
about the idea of the "Tree of Life." To some it's an abstract
idea used to teach concepts to followers of the faith, to others
it's a physical tree, hidden away like the Christian Holy Grail.
Joey Korn believes the Tree of Life is a real thing, and he
knows where it is. "The Tree of Life is a tangible pattern of
energies around every person. That's become a hallmark of
my work, and it all ties back into Judaism."

Korn has a photo taken by his mother-in-law in Israel shortly
after the country had reclaimed some land from Jordan. The
Jordanians had paved over a cemetery, and the photo shows a
Hasidic Rabbi dowsing to find the gravesites so the bodies
could be exhumed and moved to a proper burial location.

"There are allusions to that [the practive of dowsing] throughout the Hebrew scriptural stories," Rabbi Gershon Winkler
told me. "There's a legend about Moses and how he got his

magic stick. He wanted to marry one of Jethro's daughters, and Jethro said nobody marries my daughter except the one who can locate and remove the staff of the first human being, which is embedded in the lake. And then Moses used a dowsing ritual, found it, and pulled it out, and that became his magic stick.

"There are a lot of stories where people are engaging the place or the space, like in our ancestor Jacob. When he was out in the wilderness on his own, it says *Vayifga ba'makom*—he encountered a place. He had to choose a place spiritually where he would have his vision of the ladder and angels going up and down."

"So there's nothing in Judaism that would forbid dowsing or divining with rods?" I asked.

"Someone showed me a photo of an ancient synagogue that they had uncovered in Israel in the North," Winkler said. "What they found on the floor of the synagogue was a whole diagram of dowsing. It's not anything that's antithetical to what we practice."

Thy rod and thy staff is a theme that comes up repeatedly in Bible verse. These objects are indicative of ruling, such as a king's scepter, and of leading, such as a shepherd's staff. These aren't necessarily just symbols. People believed the objects held power in and of themselves. Or possibly these objects helped channel and focus our own power.

"The staff was very powerful and very important in our tradition," Rabbi Winkler said. "It was something that a teacher would give to their disciple and probably because of the power of dowsing, or what we call dowsing."

Water diversion is another mystical practice associated with dowsing. Many dowsers claim that water can be moved through focused intent. A vein of water can be opened and made to run to an area where it is needed, provided it's close enough and the person trying to move the water is psychically strong enough to do so.

This practice of diversion is also ancient. In the Bible, Moses's sister Miriam was known to draw water from the earth. When Moses struck the rock in Exodus, was he finding water or drawing water to him? The end result is obviously the same—his people don't die of thirst. And in the story of when Moses led the Jews from Egypt, he parted the Red Sea—the ultimate act of water diversion.

For Joey Korn, dowsing is an invaluable tool for finding and mapping patterns of energies, and the practice is most definitely spiritual. Finding energies with dowsing is no different than finding underground water or minerals. There are reasons that places of religious significance stand where they are today. Whether someone walked around with a forked stick and said, "Place the altar here," or whether they simply sensed that a specific location was important because of a feeling they had inside makes no difference. With focused intent, they found what they sought.

"Intent is what affects change," Korn said. "We are putting our thoughts, actions, and emotions—our intent—into our living environment energetically every moment of every day. So most of us are unconsciously filling ourselves and surrounding ourselves energetically with what we fear, with our anger, with our negative emotions. You can take charge of that process and knowingly surround yourself and fill yourself with the intent of what you want to bring into your life, rather than what you don't want to bring."

Korn became a fervent dowser. He discovered energy patterns everywhere he brought his L-rods. But it was at an American Society of Dowsers conference in Vermont in 1994 that really broadened his horizons as to what is possible with dowsing. "In 1994, I really saw what many other people were doing with dowsing," he said. "And I said, 'Man, this is unlimited!'"

Detrimental energies are the energy patterns Korn is seeking. Why? By identifying these detrimental energies, he believes he can change them through prayer. He spoke about cases where he's dowsed a house where a person lived who had cancer. The person had colon cancer, and Korn describes finding negative streams of energy intersecting right at this man's bed and in the spot where his lower portion would be when sleeping. Considering we sleep about one-third of our lives, Korn believes ensuring our beds are free of detrimental energy is critical to a good night's rest and general healthy well-being.

To demonstrate these detrimental energies, Korn walked me through a dowsing lesson over the phone. He asked if I was near a computer. My office actually has three of them. I told him I have a large, desktop monitor in front of me now.

"First of all, know you can dowse," he said.

I do believe I can dowse. Dowsing never seemed that mysterious to me in the first place. In the basic instructions included with the dowsing roads I purchased, Joey Korn recommends a few basics for using the rods: Position your arms at a relaxed bend and hold the handles comfortably in front of you. To keep the rods parallel in front of me, I needed to point the tips down slightly so gravity held them in place. I now had the rods in the ready position in front of me—like two copper pistols. "I'm ready," I told him.

"Imagine there are bands of detrimental energy radiating out from the computer screen," he said. "Not in straight lines, but curved bands. You're going to think, 'Show me detrimental energies that might be radiating out from that computer,' and you're going to walk forward and expect the response when you enter that energy."

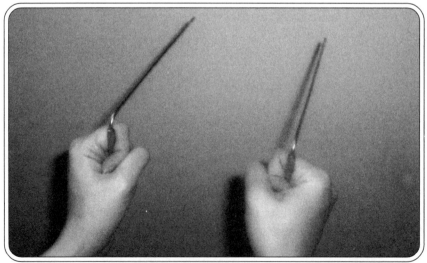

The dowsing rods in the parallel search position. Photo by Jeff Belanger.

"Say out loud, 'I want my rods to cross to find energies radiating from appliances,'" Korn said. "Tilt your hands inward very slowly so the rods move in a controlled way and make an X."

I did. They formed the X.

"Now say, 'Like this,'" he said.

I repeated him.

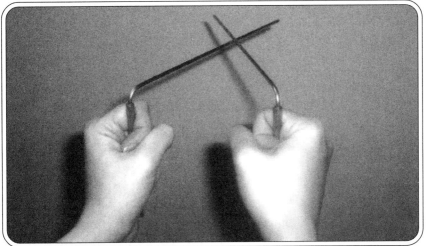

The dowsing rods, crossed, in the full dowsing reaction position. Photo by Jeff Belanger.

"You're training your body to get this dowsing response to a certain kind of energy," Korn said.

I let the rods go back to the ready position, and I backed up about 6 feet from my computer monitor. I slowly walked toward the monitor while thinking about energy waves coming off of it. It wasn't too difficult to imagine detrimental energy emitting from my screen. After many long days of working in front of the computer, I know from my aching eyes that there is bad radiation nearby.

Once I got within a foot of the monitor, the rods crossed. I told Korn of my results and kept the rods where they were— crossed in front of the monitor.

"When you get right on top of the monitor, that's the strongest band," he said. "Tell yourself this is detrimental energy that radiates from appliances. Now say a blessing. Say something like 'Dear God,' or however you address the divine, 'Change all of the energies from this equipment to be beneficial to me.'"

I listened closely as Korn said his blessing, and I repeated it to myself. The rods uncrossed and went back to the search position.

Was the rods' response psychosomatic? Maybe. But I can promise I didn't move my hands. There is a real physical factor—the monitor—and I know from eye-straining experience, news reports, and magazine articles that it does emit radiation. If I believe I have cleansed that radiation and somehow made myself immune to it, then the end certainly justifies the means. Does it make scientific sense? Not necessarily, but not everything has a scientific explanation.

The difference between spirit communication and divination is a fine line. In divining, you're using supernatural means to try and determine the future. Spirit communication involves specific messages from or even a conversation with a being or beings who are not on the same physical plane as we are.

Reaching out to spirits is something many people do through dowsing, but sometimes the spirits reach out to us even if we aren't looking. Ray Machell claims to frequently encounter spirits when dowsing. "What happens is, we come across them when we're dowsing, and we can't dowse properly until they're gone. They do affect us."

"How can you tell that spirits are present when dowsing for water?" I asked.

"When my wife and I dowse, I'll start at one end of the property and she'll start at the other and we'll both end up at the same spot exactly. So if we go on a piece of property and she gets [a dowsing reading of] 125 feet and I get 270 feet, and she gets four gallons per minute and I get 19, then our next question for the rods is, 'Is there something on this property that's affecting us?'

"So then we dowse to find out what it is and we clear it."

To clear the spirits, Machell also employs prayer.

There is one dowsing device that can be used for more specific messages in regards to spirit communication. The pendulum can be used in conjunction with a letter chart to point out letters, thus spelling out words. By holding the pendulum above the chart, the user allows the pendulum to be drawn to different sections of the chart to signify answers. With a letter chart, the dowser waits for a reaction over the specific letter and then notes the message as it unfolds. This sounds very similar to a talking or Ouija board—though the planchette is replaced by the pendulum. Ray Machell is vehemently against spirit boards because he believes users open themselves up to any being who wants to communicate—and that could be something bad. However, he does regularly employ pendulum dowsing with charts to get messages.

"So what is the difference between using a Ouija board and dowsing over a chart with the pendulum?" I asked. "Would a person be just as susceptible?"

"Most people who use Ouija boards do so as a game and do not realize what can come in," Machell said. "If a person is a dowser, or deals with the metaphysical, they will probably be familiar with the methods of protecting themselves so as to allow only what is for their greatest and highest good to come in and keep everything else out. This should *always* be done with any forms of accessing the unknown, no matter what tool is used."

Pendulum dowsing is something I've experienced before and didn't even realize it. The concept was shown to me by my mother-in-law and was something she's toyed with since childhood. Here's how to do it: Thread a needle as if you were going to sew something and make sure you have a good 10 inches or so from the needle to the end of the thread. Hold the thread in one hand and let the needle hang over the open palm of your free hand. Now think "circles," and you'll notice the needle will move in a circular motion over your palm. Now think "back and forth," and you'll see the needle move back and forth. This is pendulum dowsing at the most basic level. The pendulum—in this case, a needle—follows your intent.

The first time I tried this little experiment, I thought it was a neat trick. The skeptic in me also must point out that an elliptical motion and a back-and-forth motion could be about the same, depending on your perspective. Because my mindset is "circle," I may construe the motion as a circle. If I switch to "back and forth," I may be subliminally predisposed to see a back-and-forth motion. It's still a very easy and neat exercise to try. Even understanding how it may be working, I can't help but notice circles or back-and-forth motions depending on what I "wish" for.

The needle and thread is just one simple pendulum. You can use anything meaningful to create your own, be it a crystal, coin, or other weighted object. It helps if the object comes to a point.

I've created a pendulum chart that I used for my own spirit communication experiment. Feel free to use it if you also want to try. There is no standard way to do this. I designed my chart because this layout made more sense to me than other charts I had seen. The most important aspect to pendulum work is to define what the motions mean at the beginning of a session. If you're using a chart such as mine, with the motions already defined, this isn't necessary. If you're not using a chart, it is common for pendulum users to verbally define the movements. For example, say, "Front-to-back motion indicates 'yes,' and side-to-side motion indicates 'no.'"

For my pendulum, I used a thin gold chain with a small golden charm at the end that belonged to my paternal grand-mother. She died in 1985. I figured, because the necklace was hers, I'd try to contact her. I set my printed chart on my desk and, with my elbow resting next to the chart, I positioned the pendulum over the black dot in the center of the chart. Once it was motionless, I raised the charm about an inch above the paper. The first question I asked was, "Is my grandmother watching over me?"

After about two to three seconds, the pendulum began to swing left to right (yes)—at first maybe 1/2 inch in each direc-tion, but it soon gained momentum until it swung about 1 inch off of center in both directions. It occurred to me that the nature of my question made this divination. I was asking a question of no one in particular, or maybe one would say I asked the universe. My next question would be spirit communication: "Grandma, are you watching over me?"

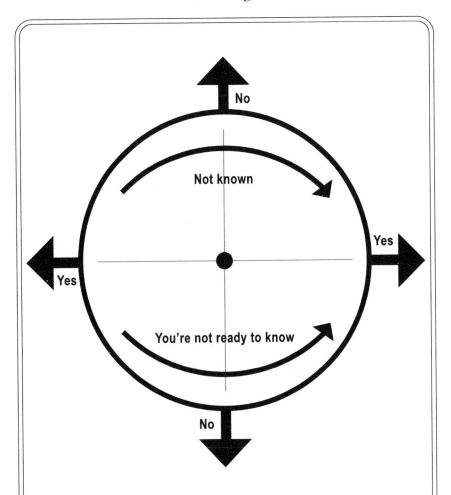

The black spot in the center represents the starting point for your pendulum and also offers a spot on which to focus during your session. The faint vertical and horizontal lines are there to help determine the swing of the pendulum. A north/south movement indicates a no answer, a left/right movement indicates a yes answer, clockwise motion means the answer is "not known," and counterclockwise means "you're not ready to know" the answer.

Within two seconds, the pendulum swung left to right again, though this time not as far—maybe 1/4 inch to 1/2 inch off of center.

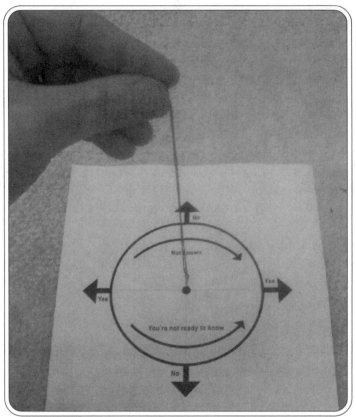

My dowsing chart and pendulum. Photo by Jeff Belanger.

I decided I needed a control to my experiment. The next question I asked: "Was I born on the planet Pluto?"

I started the same way as before, and within a second or two, my pendulum began to swing north and south, indicating no. There was one more experiment I wanted to try. I again asked my grandmother if she was watching over me. The pendulum swung in a clockwise, then counterclockwise direction, then finally settled in a left-to-right motion indicating yes. While it was swinging, I asked again, "Was I born on the planet Pluto?"

The pendulum continued to swing left-to-right. I asked again if I was born on Pluto, but the pendulum continued to swing left-to-right. So my experiment was a bit inconclusive. As one more control to my experiment, I tried simply holding the pendulum without asking any questions. I wanted to test whether the chain would naturally start to swing on its own. I held my hand steady for a full minute, and though there was the tiniest bit of movement, the pendulum never swung out any further than the edge of the central black dot.

I spoke with more expert dowsers who said stopping the pendulum after each answer may be a good idea for a beginner. Others also suggested that beginners may need to actually start the pendulum swinging themselves to get it going.

I don't have the "start up" problem. It certainly is a peculiar feeling watching the pendulum gain momentum and force even though I'm keeping my hand as steady as possible.

A week after my first experiment, I tried again and asked the following six questions, stopping the pendulum after each answer:

1. Grandma, are you still watching over me?
   Left-right swing, indicating yes.
2. Is my name Jeff?
   Left-right swing, indicating yes.
3. Have I ever been to the South Pole?
   Forward-backward swing, indicating no.
4. Is spirit communication possible through the pendulum?
   Left-right swing, indicating yes.
5. Is world peace possible?
   Clockwise motion, indicating "not known."
6. Are there any spirits present in this room with me right now?
   Counterclockwise motion, indicating "you're not ready to know."

I can't disagree with any of the answers. I can confirm that I haven't been to the South Pole and that my name is Jeff. The other answers require a leap of faith. I was impressed that each control question was answered correctly. I also noticed that with some answers, the motion was more pronounced. For example, question 6 delivered a very large circular motion—was someone making it extra clear I'm not ready to know?

Maureen Wood is a psychic investigator with the New England Ghost Project (NEGP) (*www.neghostproject.com*), and she's been a member of the American Society of Dowsers since 1999. The 41-year-old, based in Andover, Massachusetts, has been dowsing since she was a teenager, though she wasn't using any dowsing tools back then and she didn't even know there was a term for what she was doing. Today, dowsing is a standard tool in NEGP's ghost investigations.

"Let's say you get this twinge in your gut every time a certain event takes place," Wood said. "If it's a positive event and you're getting this intuition or this twinge in your gut every time, you start linking things up. You need to be in tune with your body—so it's an internal dowsing tool."

Wood uses pendulum dowsing (she has both a crystal and a copper one) as part of her paranormal investigations.

"How do you incorporate the pendulum?" I asked.

"Even if you use the pendulum, I think you still have to use your psychic ability," she said. "So we'll go into the establishment, and Ron [Ron Kolek, NEGP founder], his son, and then a few other members will go around with the scientific equipment. They'll take their EMF meters, they'll set up the temperature gauges, and they'll walk around the establishment and try to map it out first. And I'll walk around with them to see if I can pick up some of the energy that's in various locations."

"So either one of you might find the energy first?" I asked.

"Right. If I sense that, yes, there is energy, Ron will usually use his meter and verify that he's also picking it up or he's not. Regardless, what I'll do is try to connect. So I'll start using the pendulum, and I'll ask yes and no questions. I may ask, 'Is there an entity present tonight?'"

For Wood, the pendulum acts as a visual point of reference for the rest of the members of her group. She may receive the answers psychically, but the rest of the group can watch the pendulum swing counterclockwise for yes, clockwise for no, and back and forth for maybe.

One of her most significant experiences with pendulum dowsing during an investigation came at the Tenney Gate House in Methuen, Massachusetts. The Gate House was built in the 1830s by William Whittier, but it was transformed into more of a Queen Anne–style house in 1883 when it was bought by millionaire Charles H. Tenney. Today, the building is home to the Metheun Historical Society and is full of artifacts and old photographs of people from throughout Metheun's history. During the NEGP's investigation, the group gathered in a hallway adjacent to several of the open rooms and Wood pulled out her citrine crystal pendulum. "When we were asking questions, I was sensing the energy and Ron was getting a reading [with his EMF meter]," she said. "I asked, 'Did you live here?' and we got a yes. I asked, 'Did you die here?' and it was a no. I said, 'If your picture is here, can you show us who you are?' The pendulum swung to the right directing us into one of the rooms."

Inside the room were many photographs of different people. Finding the exact photo would take more dowsing. The NEGP walked into the room and Wood continued. "I said, 'Can you show me who you are amongst these people?' And it definitely swung right toward a picture of this gentleman. Then we started making a connection with him. I started feeling chest pains and numbness in my arm. As it turned out, that was the gentleman who owned the home and he was believed to have died of a heart attack. There were a few other pictures there, but he was the one who owned the place and had the same kind of illness. So we were able to get some proof on the reading."

In the Tenney Gate House basement, Wood again used the pendulum to try and establish contact. But this time, the pendulum wasn't moving in a natural motion. "If you're holding a pendulum, it goes in a circle, either counterclockwise or clockwise or it doesn't even move at all," she said. "We watched the stone [pendulum] actually move in an X-shape. Everybody could see it, not just me. I felt the energy—it was there. I

asked Ron to put his EMF reader underneath the stone because I could feel somebody lifting up the weight of it, and the
meter was blaring under the stone. When we were done, Ron
asked if he could take a look at the stone. He picked it up and
started looking at it, and the stone itself was all fractured. The
energy that was there was really intense because it basically
ran fractures all through the stone."

There are indeed energies all around us—electromagnetic
fields from our planet, the wires in our walls, radiation from
solar flares, and many other power sources that can crisscross
our paths. Many religious traditions believe everything has a
spirit—the rock, the trees, and us. If everything has a life
energy to it that constantly interacts with the natural energies
of our planet and of our universe, then dowsing can help us find
those power sources. If some of the energies are intelligent and
interactive, then dowsing is a valid tool to open ourselves up to
those communication channels.

"The first time it happens, you will drop the pen. Everybody does, because you say,

'Wow, it's happening!' And then you might as well quit, because you'll be so excited that you won't be able to get back into it. So try again the next day."

Automatic Writing

Imagine putting your pen to paper and watching the words appear on the page. Though it's your hand, the handwriting isn't your own, and you have no thoughts or control over what is being written. The concept of automatic writing pushes the idea of mediumship a bit further than many other spirit communication devices. A talking board, a deck of tarot cards, or even a camera enables us to mostly remove our bodies from the equation. We put a physical barrier between ourselves and the "spirit world," and we can claim—even if only for our own sanity—that the object was the medium, not us. But with automatic writing, we put our bodies even closer to the action. With only a pen or pencil between us and the mysterious force, for anything coherent to come of the exercise, *we* must become the medium. We have to relinquish control of our hand to an otherworldly influence. This begins to move into the realm of spirit possession—an idea that should certainly raise an eyebrow.

Automatic writing, like many other spirit communication methods we've discussed, was born of the Spiritualist movement. There are a few vague references to the use of automatic writing in various royal courts some centuries earlier, but nothing concrete. Additionally, most people were illiterate centuries ago. Literacy levels in the United States didn't start a dramatic rise until the second half of the 19th century; the further back in history we go, the lower the literacy levels drop. Even for those who were literate, pens and ink were a luxury item, so only the well-off could afford to experiment with automatic writing—assuming they had ever even heard of the idea.

We know that Kate Fox practiced automatic writing, as her and her sister's fame—and their following—grew after those first knocks on the wall in 1848. According to Barbara Weisberg's book, *Talking to the Dead*, people were gathering in mini social clubs to explore this phenomenon. In 1850, a group that called itself the New York Circle, founded by Charlotte Fowler Wells, held weekly gatherings to try and commune with spirits. Horace Greeley, founder and editor of the *New York Tribune* and a bit of a celebrity himself, was known to stop by the New York Circle, and occasionally he brought Kate Fox with him. Wells's brother, Edward Fowler, became a medium who would put himself into a trancelike state to communicate with spirits, and he often employed automatic writing in these sessions; his hand would write out messages from the other side on blank sheets of paper. Allegedly, Fowler sometimes wrote messages in languages foreign to him, other sessions offered cryptic symbols or hieroglyphs, and on some occasions, words appeared on the paper without any human intervention at all.

There are a variety of experiences that can be considered part of automatic writing, ranging from the subtle to the extreme. On the most subtle end of this spectrum, we have stream-of-consciousness writing—something many people have experienced, myself included. Some writers may call this "the muse descending"; others may use a sports analogy and say they're "in the zone." Stream of consciousness is the point when you know exactly what you want to write and the words seem to pour out of you like microbrewed beer from a tap. I can recall several occasions when I've been writing and suddenly realize that I've typed a page or more without even breaking my thought. I had no sense of time, and when I became aware of how much I had written, I had little recollection of what I had just typed until I read it again—as if my fingers were typing as fast or faster than my brain thought of the words. Sometimes the ideas are a bit disjointed when written this way, but nothing an editor can't fix. Some writers have published entire books written in stream of consciousness. One such tome I vividly remember struggling through in college was William Faulkner's 1929 novel, *The Sound and the Fury*. Here's a gem from Faulkner's book to give you an example:

> She smelled like trees. In the corner it was dark, but I could see the window. I squatted there, holding the slipper. I couldn't see it, but my hands saw it, and I could hear it getting night, and my hands saw the slipper but I couldn't see myself but my hands could see the slipper, and I squatted there, hearing it getting dark."

In reading Faulkner's words again, I have the same thoughts I did the first time: "Huh?" But this passage is an excellent example of what happens when every fleeting thought of your conscious (and maybe part of your subconscious) mind makes it to paper. This is by no means traditional automatic writing, but stream-of-consciousness writing is tapping into something very close. In reading a stream-of-consciousness message and putting that message into the context of our own lives, we may get some idea of meaning. Like many enigmatic messages, the exact connotation will vary based on who is reading and interpreting the content.

This early stage is where some people first discover automatic writing. Through working with the practice, stream of consciousness can evolve to stream of unconsciousness, where you're either communicating with your subconscious mind, your higher self, or possibly the spirit world.

Author and Witch Edain McCoy wrote a book in 1994 called *How to Do Automatic Writing*. I spoke to her from her home in central Indiana. The 47-year-old has written many books on Witchcraft, magic, and spellcasting. When we spoke, her Sheltie, Corky, barked hello in the background.

McCoy told me her first experience with automatic writing happened during a seminar run by Dick and Tara Sutphen in Sedona, Arizona, in the mid-1980s. McCoy was 29 years old at the time and was trying to conceive a child with her husband. Sadly, she had already suffered two miscarriages and was trying to conceive again when she attended the seminar. "I had wheat lying around the bed, and tarot cards with crystals all around it," McCoy said. "It just looked crazy in there."

At the seminar, the roughly 300 attendees were told to find someone they'd never met before, only exchange names and where they were from, and to go find a quiet spot to sit face-to-face and knee-to-knee.

"She was Evelyn from California, I was Edain from Texas," McCoy said. "We went out and we sat by the pool. It was nice Arizona weather, the pool was lukewarm, the chairs were vinyl and sticky, and I couldn't even get into an altered state at that point."

"Was this simply a psychic experiment?" I asked.

"We were supposed to be getting information from each others' spirit guides," she said. The messages from the spirit guides were then supposed to be written down. "It didn't help looking up and seeing Evelyn just scribbling away."

"So you had a hard time connecting, so to speak?"

"Definitely. I just tried to mentally cast a circle and get myself centered. And I was finally getting some impressions of her as being isolated and alone. And some impressions about her marriage—that she didn't have to sacrifice it to pursue her separate interests. I just went with it because that's what I was feeling. And I thought, I can't tell somebody I just met and don't know something like this. She was probably 55 to 60 and I was a smart-ass 29-year-old."

When Evelyn and Edain stopped writing, Edain gave her reading first. "I told her everything I wrote, and I was stunned that it made sense to her." Evelyn said she felt alone and went on to explain how her husband was on a Caribbean cruise while she had come to Sedona with some women she didn't even know that well.

Next it was Evelyn's turn to share her reading. "I was thinking that I was going to get one of those little poetic things," McCoy said. "You know, plant your garden in your heart and watch love grow." I laughed with McCoy as she recounted. "And her first words—and I don't remember anything else beyond those—were, 'So when are you going to ask me about the baby?'

This message was supposed to be from my spirit guide. Well, I had to pull my jaw up off my chest."

"Were you conscious of what you were writing at the time?" I asked.

"I was mostly but not completely conscious when I was writing. I don't know whether she was or not. As long as the impressions and the words are coming, then you don't stop," she said.

This first experience led McCoy into deeper study of automatic writing. She would write a single question at the top of a page—often the nature of her questions were about help or guidance with issues in her life at the time. "Who answers the question?" I asked.

"I'm either asking my higher self to work as a medium or I'm reaching out to a loved one. Kind of like you would with any oracle—you don't want to bring anything into you, you want that barrier, but you still want information from another being."

"With other oracles, like tarot or talking boards, that barrier is definitely more prominent," I said. "Is automatic writing as safe as the other oracles?"

"I think it's always safest to allow your higher self to work as a medium—your crown chakra—because to me it's just crazy not to. I would never use the Ouija board without protection either. I've never had a problem with automatic writing. I've heard secondhand stories from people, like hands just wouldn't stop moving, or pens flew around the room, and all of this crazy stuff, but nobody can substantiate any of this."

McCoy believes she successfully used automatic writing to contact her grandmother. "I'm a show-me person, though I'm not from Missouri," she said and then laughed. "My grandmother came through and I just knew it was her, but I had to have a proof. I said, 'Tell me something only you and I would know.' When she was alive, we would sit on the bed like two 12-year-olds and talk about things—she told me a lot of secrets. At the time, she had said that now that my grandfather was gone, no one else in the world knew. And she told me a few of those secrets [through automatic writing] and I said, 'Okay, you're Granny!'"

We talked about what people need to do to prepare for automatic writing. She said the state of mind needed is a bit deeper compared to tarot cards or runes. She suggested finding a quiet and private place. "In fact, I suggest in my book—go to the bathroom," she said. "People think that's funny, but where else in most people's homes do you not usually have a window to the outside? You have darkness, you have a place you can set a candle where you don't have to worry about it falling over and burning anything, and you have a door you can shut and lock, and people respect it. The bathroom is the perfect place."

"I know I get all of my best ideas in there!" I said.

"Sure! Most of us do," she said.

Within a quiet, private place, you want to relax and put your pen to paper. Some people who teach automatic writing suggest you start by writing what you're thinking or simply drawing letters, the idea being that this will turn into stream of consciousness and then into automatic writing. "I had trouble starting that way," McCoy said. "Because writing words or letters suggested that I was triggering sentences in my head. So I would just make flowing signs on the paper, or the only things I might write in terms of words were, 'write, write, write.'"

"How do you know when it's working?" I asked.

"The first time it happens, you will drop the pen," she said. "Everybody does, because you say, 'Wow, it's happening!' And then you might as well quit, because you'll be so excited that you won't be able to get back into it. So try again the next day."

On Ghostvillage.com's message board community, I asked if anyone had ever tried automatic writing and, if so, what results did they get. Nicole Hanna from Fairhaven, Michigan, sent me a note about her introduction to automatic writing. I gave her a call at her house; the 28-year-old's Southern accent let me know she was not a Michigan native. "Nope, I'm from Arkansas," she said.

Hanna first heard about automatic writing around 11 years of age. "I had had a few encounters with a Ouija board, and that kind of pushed me into the field of paranormal studies," she said. "I would head to the bookstore to find out anything I could and eventually ran across pendulum work, automatic writing, and different forms of spirit communication. I never actually attempted to try automatic writing out myself; it just sort of happened."

"What do you mean?" I asked.

"This was years after I had first read about it. I was probably 19 at the time and sitting in class on campus, just minding my own business, and all of a sudden I just kind of zoned out. I don't remember what the rest of the class was about. I kind of snapped out of it when everybody was leaving for the day, and I looked down at my paper and I just had a sheet full of scribbles."

"Was anything legible?" I asked.

"It was completely legible. It just seemed like disjointed thoughts, but the writing was completely legible; you could see everything and understand everything."

Hanna doesn't have the original messages anymore, but she said the gist of the message was along the lines of her not being alone, that the spirit who did the writing was always with her. She said that about a week before this accidental automatic writing session happened, she had been exploring the idea of spirit guides and guardian angels. She was skeptical of the idea until she got her answer in writing. In the original message, and in some following automatic writing sessions, the spirit identified himself as "Michael"—a name that didn't hold any significance to Hanna.

This first experience launched many future attempts at contact. "For the most part, I was pretty conscious of what was going on, and I made an effort not to look at what was being written," she said. "Because I'm always afraid that your mind will project what it wants in the session and create its own thing. So I just kind of let it go and see where it goes from there."

In some sessions, Hanna would ask specific questions seeking advice for situations she was facing in her life at that time. On other occasions she feels that she sensed the presence of a spirit near her and she sought to contact that spirit in the session. And sometimes she would put the pen to paper and just see what came out.

For her sessions, she made herself comfortable at a desk, placed the pen to paper, relaxed, and waited. On some occasions, the writing started almost immediately. Other times it might have taken 10 minutes before words started to form, and the pace of the writing would be so slow that a single word could take several minutes to complete.

"Are you conscious of your hand moving during this?" I asked.

"Yes, I'm really conscious of it because it's kind of a bizarre feeling," she said. The last time she tried automatic writing was around 2000. She said she was unsuccessful in her last attempt and hasn't gone back to the idea since, though our conversation did re-ignite her interest in the practice.

On December 9, 2004, at 1:20 p.m., a few days after we spoke, Hanna tried automatic writing again. She said she was fully rested, her household chores were completed, and the house was quiet—no radios, televisions, washers, or dryers were running. It's worth noting that her house does have a history of paranormal activity such as cabinet doors slamming on their own, at all hours of the day and night; children's toys turning themselves on and off, even when they don't have batteries in them; voices whispering; and strong smells emanating from isolated spots.

During this attempt, Hanna asked a series of questions and received short answers to those questions. Here is the transcript she provided me:

> Are you a spirit of the light?
> yes
>
> Are you male or female?
> female
>
> What is your name?
> meredith
>
> Why are you here?
> [couldn't understand writing]

This first session lasted approximately 15 minutes. After a 10-minute break, she attempted contact again:

Is Meredith still with me?
yes

Are you my spirit guide?
no

Are you a resident of this house?
yes

Did you live here before?
no

How did you come to be here?
I followed you

From where?
Arkansas

Why?
watch

Watch what?
spirits follow you

Why?
you see them

Is there a message for me?
not at this time.

The second session also lasted 15 minutes. The following day, Hanna tried again and achieved a more significant message. In the 10-minute automatic writing session, she didn't ask any specific questions, she just waited for a message. In the following, all spelling, punctuation, and grammar mistakes have been preserved. This is an exact transcript of the session on December 10, 2004, at 8 p.m.; Hanna's comments on what was happening appear in brackets:

Tomorrow the sun sets deeply and there will be rest for the wicked and the light seems brighter from the other side and no one feels but the pain and happiness they inflict upon their enemies. [long pause] kindess is the way to restful death [The pen trailed here. I began again on a new sheet of paper.]

The message continued as follows:

> Rotten disappears briefly in sweet realizing eternity burns slowly with siner madness circles we perpetuate with our actions and cosmic disappointment when fears tell who we are [long pause] sounds echo our hearts in death as do the choices we make when we die so chose well and with no blind eye sufer [suffer?] not...[the pen trailed off the sheet. I tried again, but got nothing.]

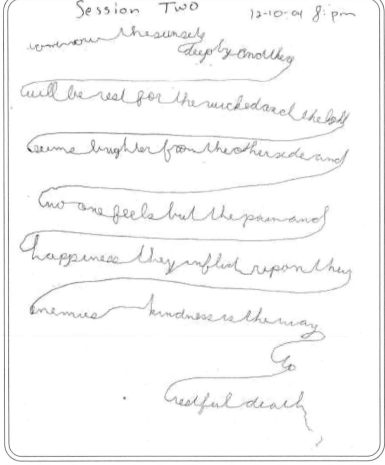

Nicole Hanna's second automatic writing sessions from December 10, 2004, at 8 p.m. Image courtesy of Nicole Hanna.

Hanna's husband, Bill, also tried an automatic writing session. Notice the striking similarities in the handwriting done by two different people on the same day.

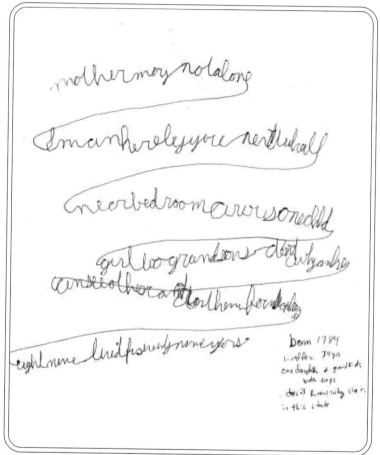

Bill Hanna's automatic writing example done the same day as Nicole's. Image courtesy of Nicole Hanna.

Tatiacha Bhodsvatan has been running the Website *www.SpiritNexus.org* since 1999, which houses a vast collection of transcripts from some of her many automatic writing sessions spanning from 1989 to 1999. I spoke to her from her home in Pagosa Springs, Colorado.

Bhodsvatan had heard about automatic writing as a child, but the 41-year-old never thought to give it a try until the late 1980s. She was learning meditation and self-hypnosis from some of Dick Sutphen's audio- and videotapes. When her mom and brother went to a Dick and Tara Sutphen seminar to learn automatic writing, among other things, Bhodsvatan's connection to the other side began to open. "While they were at the seminar, I had this experience where I was sitting on my couch and all of a sudden it was like being in a loud coffee shop with all of the clanking of dishes and voices talking, and I somehow knew that there was something different going on," she said. "I guess I was sort of in a trance without really knowing it at the time, because I didn't have a lot of experience. I received the letters of the name of my spirit guide. I just received these letters one at a time."

"You received the letters psychically?" I asked.

"They were just in my mind like all of a sudden B–E...so I wrote it down and stuck it on my refrigerator and I somehow was convinced that when my brother and mom came back from the seminar that they would know what it meant," Bhodsvatan said. "I don't know why I thought that. So when they came back, I said, 'Here, I have this piece of paper and it has these letters and you guys know what it means, right?' And they said, 'No. Why would we know what that means?'"

This would be a sample of my normal handwriting

A sample of Tatiacha Bhodsvatan's handwriting. Image courtesy of Tatiacha Bhodsvatan.

Bhodsvatan's mother and brother told her how they learned automatic writing at the seminar by drawing a series of many circles on a piece of paper to try and put themselves into a trance. Bhodsvatan didn't know how to get into a trance, but she was determined to have a full automatic writing experience. She used one of the Sutphens' videotapes to get herself close to a trancelike state, and then a paragraph written by her spirit guide flowed through her hand. The name that signed the paper was the same name she received in her first vision: Bestali.

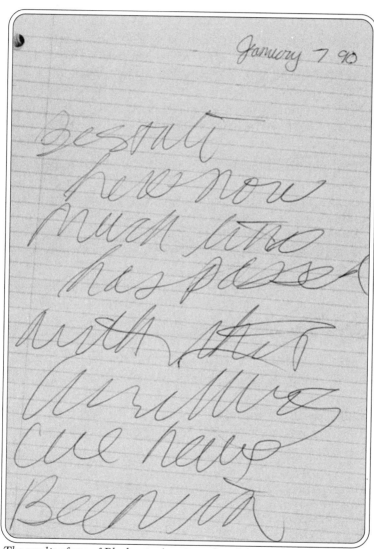

The results of one of Bhodsvatan's automatic writing sessions, from January 7, 1990, with her spirit guide, Bestali. The text says, "Bestali here now, much time has passed with this writing, we have been in...." Image courtesy of Tatiacha Bhodsvatan.

"I was really excited," she said. "He said that he was my guide and everything was okay. He also said there's another one here too, Samantha."

"Did you know who he meant?" I asked.

"I had a baby that was stillborn, who I named Samantha. I think he brought her into that very first automatic writing session because that was kind of my impetus to get through any fear. I wanted to know why she didn't come to me, why she chose to go back to spirit. That burning desire to know the answer to that question was more than the fear I had of doing the writing itself. It basically said that she was there and she was with me."

In the coming months and years, Bhodsvatan used automatic writing up to several times per day and found the words came as fast as her hand could keep up. "The writing would be really huge, and I also realized very quickly that I couldn't use pens," she said. "The energy was so strong that the ink would dry up in the pens. I finally realized I needed to use pencils." And using notebooks was also too cumbersome considering the pace she was writing at. Bhodsvatan switched to plain typing paper. Before each session, she numbered the pages so as each sheet filled she could throw it off the desk and start the next sheet. Once the communication was over, she would pick up all of the pages and put them back in order.

On her Website, Bhodsvatan lists a host of spirit entities that she has communicated with through automatic writing. One name definitely jumped out at me. "I see from your list that you've made contact with Jesus," I said. "Do you consider yourself Christian?"

"I'm definitely not a Christian," she said. "I don't have anything against Christianity, I just consider Jesus one of the great teachers out of many. The time that I connected with him was actually very short. They [the spirits] were introducing me to a lot of different ascended beings, and I was discovering the commonality between them and the ways that they taught. There were a couple of communications that came through with Jesus and they just wanted me to feel his energy."

Considering how often the name Sutphen came up in my discussions about automatic writing, I definitely wanted to connect with the people who are teaching so many others how to do this. I spoke with Tara Sutphen from her home in Malibu, California. Sutphen first learned automatic writing from her husband, Dick, in 1983. "I seemed to be naturally really good at it," she told me.

Sutphen's interest and work in the spirit world began when she was 8 years old and had a near-death experience after an accident left her hemorrhaging. Sutphen remembers being on the operating table and then recalls being above her body— almost as if she wanted to get out of the way of the doctors and nurses who were working on her. She described how she went to the light but was told by her spirit guide that she had to go back.

Automatic writing, she would discover years later, was a very specific way for her to connect with spirits. It was through automatic writing that she learned that name of her guide: Abenda.

"How do you begin an automatic writing session?" I asked.

"I have a system where I meet my spirit guide," Sutphen said. "I'm in my temple room, I go out into the astral plane where we have a glass teahouse, and then we [she and her spirit guide] invite people in to write." (The glass teahouse is an ethereal place as opposed to a physical place.)

Sutphen claims she received more than 900 letters in 2003 from people requesting her to make contact for them and to get answers through automatic writing. She became the medium for those people—kind of a supernatural Postmaster General. "If I got a letter from you," Sutphen said, "or if I wanted information for you, I would go to the glass teahouse. Whoever comes for you to write will write through my hand."

The letters flowed and she mailed the responses back to each person who sent in questions. She claims the handwriting was different depending on the spirit, and many different languages have also come forward—languages where she would have to seek the help of a translator to understand. Today, she no longer does automatic writing for others, because she said she was spending more time in the spirit world than ours. She had to stop to get balance back.

For Sutphen, her spirit guide is a critical part of automatic writing. She recommends that we all try and connect with our own spirit guides, though the nature of what you ask for from your guide shouldn't be trivial.

"A few years ago we were doing a seminar in San Diego, and a woman was telling me that her spirit guide didn't come to her anymore," Sutphen said. "I said, 'What are you asking your spirit guide? Are you asking a question over and over? What exactly do you want from your spirit guide?' She said, 'I go into the parking lots at the mall and ask for a good parking space—will you give it to me?'"

"What's wrong with that?" I asked.

"Right!" she said and laughed. "It's nice to wish for that, but the bottom line is that's not really your spirit guide's job. So you're going to have to find another way to get that good parking spot."

"What keeps you coming back to this practice after so long?" I asked.

"There's no doubt that automatic writing is the most meaningful and most accurate form of spirit communication for me."

During the height of the Spiritualist movement, a device emerged to help facilitate automatic writing. The tool started as a small basket with a pencil attached to it. When the medium established contact with the spirit and touched the basket, the spirit would take over with the writing. Around 1860, the "planchette" was developed. Those familiar with Ouija or the talking board know the planchette as the pointer device used to mark each letter in the message. Before its use on the talking boards, the planchette looked very much the same—a small table made of wood about the size of your hand with three legs, though the hole in it was just big enough to push a pencil through. The user or users would gently rest their hands on the planchette and push the pencil tip down so it made a mark on the paper, and the messages would be spelled out that way. In the 1860s, Kirby and Company sold the Kirby's Planchette, a mahogany version with the instructions glued to the underside of the device.

Around 1875, game manufacturer Selchow and Righter produced a product called *Planchette: The Mystic of Mystics*. The front cover of the box featured the fingertips of two hands resting on the planchette, with a pencil poking through the hole and marking wavy lines on the paper underneath. Around the hands are three greenish phantom faces watching the hands. The maple planchette inside looks more like the modern "shield" shape we know as the planchette today.

To get one of these pencil-holding planchettes today, you'll need to search antique shops, tag sales, and auctions. As a teenager, I remember converting the planchette from my Ouija board to one that would hold a pencil by using a lot of tape. It wasn't pretty, but it did hold the pen against the paper. I remember the planchette moving when a friend and I put our hands on it, but nothing legible was spelled out.

The most extreme end of the automatic writing spectrum is spirit writing; you place a pencil and paper together, and a message is written without any human intervention at all, beyond the setup. The paper and pencil are placed in a spirit cabinet, and when the cabinet is opened, the paper may have messages written on it. Sometimes this is done by simple sleight of hand—replacing the blank sheet with a piece of paper that had messages already written on it—although some claim the experience can be genuine.

Another form of this is slate writing—a practice very popular with the Spiritualist movement in the second half of the 19th century. Mediums used a small, handheld chalkboard, and answers mystically appeared to questions asked by people in the room. Slate writing was an easy tool for charlatans to incorporate. While I can't say for certain that all slate writing was fraudulent, it seems from testimony and testing that the vast majority of slate writing was indeed faked. In some cases, the person getting the reading would sit at a table across from the "medium." After the question was asked, the medium slid the blank slate under the table, wrote on it with chalk hidden underneath, said some magic words, and pulled the slate out with alleged spirit writing on it. In other cases, the slate would be two-sided and already have some pre-written answers on one side. The slate was simply flipped over under the table to reveal the "spirit message." One has to imagine that a genuine case of spirit writing would be a life-changing event for the witness.

I decided to try my own spirit writing experiment. I took a single piece of white printer paper and a pencil and placed them on my kitchen table. I asked, "If any spirits are present, please make some kind of clear marking on the paper." I then covered the paper with an upside-down box. We'll check in with the box later.

I put a lot of stock in the written word. In general, when most people write, they try to be specific and choose the right words to express exactly what they mean. Of course, we're not always successful at expressing ourselves through writing, but we at least come close. I was eager to try automatic writing, because if a message does come through for me, then I imagine it would be meaningful.

I sat down at my desk with a blank sheet of paper and a pencil. At the top of the paper I wrote, "Hello, is anybody there?" I set the pencil in a comfortable position, relaxed my hand and arm, and faced forward. I closed my eyes as well. After about two minutes, I became very conscious of the point where the pencil met the paper. I felt as though my hand was making swirling rings, though I knew the pencil point hadn't moved. I started to feel as if my whole body was swirling in some slow centrifuge. I felt the pencil tip slide a fraction of an inch. I opened my eyes, but kept staring straight ahead. I didn't look at my hand, but I could see it in my peripheral vision.

The entire experience lasted about five minutes. My pencil had moved slightly, though nothing profound. In a second session, I attempted making a series of many circles on the page but wound up with nothing but circles.

The mark my pencil left on my first automatic writing endeavor is at the top. My circle-drawing attempt takes up the rest of the paper. Photo by Jeff Belanger.

It had been just over an hour since I left my box-covered paper and pencil on my kitchen table. When I lifted the box, nothing at all was amiss. I wasn't surprised. The concept of this kind of spirit writing is counter to all other oracles and methods of spirit communication—a human is needed as either the channel or the interpreter of the message.

Deciding which spirit communication method is right for you is, of course, an individual choice. Automatic writing is one of the closest methods to direct spirit communication that we've discussed in these pages. But for some, even this isn't direct enough. Peter James (*www.ghostencounters.com*) has been a full-time ghost hunter and psychic since 1980 and has been studying ghosts and his own psychic abilities since his first ghost encounter when he was 7 years old and living in Rochester, New York. James spent eight years as the resident psychic on the television show *Sightings*, and he is currently working on a new television show called *Ghost Encounters*. I spoke to James from his home in Los Angeles about spirit communication.

"I very much respect those who continue using methods like Ouija boards, tarot cards, séances—that kind of methodology and/or technique—but I find it all to be nothing more than a toy," James said. "What means of transportation do you have now, Jeff?"

"I have a car," I said.

"Not a horse and buggy, right? And do you have a type-writer?"

"No, I have a computer."

"See what I mean? People are still stuck way back in the 16th century. My point is that direct communication is the answer."

For Peter James, developing a means to see, hear, and speak to spirits is what we all should be striving for. Though most people—myself included—may not be ready for coming face-to-face with a ghost and saying hello.

"Remember that knowledge and identity takes the sting out of fear," he said. "The majority of people that I encounter are still dealing with fear. What if I see a ghost? What if he follows me home? What if? What if? Like most people, most ghosts are friendly. I base all of my theories and opinions on the premise of: as in life, as in death; so in life, so in death. All of the fear that people conjure up is in their head, not in reality."

I don't consider myself psychic, or even sensitive for that matter, so I find the idea of a bridge between myself and potential spirit communication appealing. But for Peter James, he believes we need to put down the scientific equipment, the channeling devices, and the automatic writing pencil, and just pay attention to our surroundings, to tune into the feelings and senses we get in a place that may have spirit activity.

People may not be attempting automatic writing in such great numbers as a few decades ago, but those who do use this form of spirit communication find it very enlightening. To be able to remove your conscious mind from the words your hand is writing and to look down and see a message written by someone else is evidence that can't be ignored for the people who do this. By saving the sessions and reading them weeks and even years after the fact, you have an immediate reconnection with what must be a very close spirit contact.

Conclusion

As our technology continues to advance at blinding speed, there's a perception among many that an experience or a thing isn't real unless we can break it down into binary 1s and 0s—computer language. This set of logic and understanding is so ingrained in all of us that we sometimes question our own senses.

In *Summa Theologica*, Thomas Aquinas writes that "music depends on arithmetic." This is certainly true. Anyone with a working finger can play piano; we can walk up to a keyboard and press the keys. But why then aren't we all Mozart? Only those with an affinity for the instrument can turn the math that is music into art. Can science explain why? No. Artists know how to speak to our emotions, to our very soul—a thing that can't be taken out, measured, or tested. But we know it's there because we have all had experiences that stir us deep inside.

If we accept the notion of an afterlife in which our spirits, personalities, and/or higher selves survive, then we must assume that communication is possible with those spirits. We must assume this based on the myriad of religious texts filled with accounts of contact with the divine over the millennia. We have to believe, based on the millions of ghost stories told throughout the world. We should know it to be true because of that thing inside all of us that makes us know beyond explanation.

This is the very edge of our human understanding and experience.

The devices used to communicate with spirits allow us to remove our rational, logical minds from the process of contact.

To those who aren't ready to believe, these things are simply games offering random results that we interpret as we see fit. When the game is over, we can put these toys back in their boxes and close off that part of our psyches until next time. To those with a more open-minded approach, the messages from these devices must be considered; whether they came from random chance or the ethereal is up to each individual to decide. Still others begin using these tools for insight but find that their own psychic abilities develop because of working with these devices.

When I began writing this book, I was intrigued by the notion of trying all of these various techniques to see what results I got. Like everyone, I have my own spiritual questions that I'm seeking answers to. I quickly realized as I started researching each topic that to get a truly profound experience requires a lot of study, dedication, and faith in yourself and the technique you're using—and a little luck doesn't hurt either.

Very few people, if any, have the "big vision" on their first attempt. But something about these devices calls to people. For some, the imagery of the tarot demands they look deeper. For others, a vision in a crystal ball offers the guidance they seek in their lives. For people who believe, these devices make the spiritual significantly more tangible. A spirit photo is something you can hold in your hand and look at again and again. A tarot or rune reading can be written down and examined for as long as you wish. When a dowsing rod moves, the person holding it has little doubt their way is about to be guided.

In Joseph Campbell's book *Myths to Live By*, he describes a conference on religion that took place in Japan. A social philosopher approaches a Japanese Shinto Priest and says, "We've been now to a good many ceremonies and have seen quite a few of your shrines. But I don't get your ideology. I don't get your theology." The Priest thinks about this for a moment and then responds, "I think we don't have ideology. We don't have theology. We dance."

The spiritual quest is a noble pursuit—and one that all of us are on, whether we're cognizant of it or not. Some choose to ignore the quest and, thus, dismiss any mystery that floats by, while others embrace it. It's important that we ask questions, important that we apply some degree of our own logic, but it's also important to dance—your spirit partners are waiting.

Bibliography

Aveni, Anthony. *Behind the Crystal Ball: Magic, Science, and the Occult from Antiquity Through the New Age.* New York: Times Books, 1996.

Bird, Christopher. *The Divining Hand: The 500 Year-Old Mystery of Dowsing.* Atglen, Pa.: Whitford Press, 2000.

Blum, Ralph H. *The Book of Runes: A Handbook for the Use of an Ancient Oracle: The Viking Runes.* New York: St. Martin's Press, 1993.

Bonner, John. *Qabalah: A Magical Primer.* Boston: Weiser Books, 1995.

Decker, Ronald. *A Wicked Pack of Cards: The Origins of the Occult Tarot.* New York: St. Martin's Press, 1996.

Estep, Sarah Wilson. *Voices of Eternity.* New York: Fawcett Gold Medal Books, 1988.

Fiery, Ann. *The Book of Divination.* San Francisco: Chronicle Books, 1999.

Fuller, John G. *The Ghost of 29 Megacycles.* New York: Signet, 1986.

Hastings, Arthur, et al. "Psychomanteum Research: Experiences and Effects on Bereavement." *Omega: Journal of Death and Dying,* 43, no. 3 (2002): 211–228.

Hawk, Ambrose. *Exploring Scrying.* Franklin Lakes, N.J.: New Page Books, 2001.

Hudson, Paul. *Mystical Origins of the Tarot: From Ancient Roots to Modern Usage.* Rochester, Vt.: Destiny Books, 2004.

Israel, Paul. *Edison: A Life of Invention.* New York: John Wiley & Sons, Inc., 1998.

Kaplan, Stuart R. *Radiant Rider-Waite Tarot Deck Instructions.* Stamford, Conn.: US Games Systems, Inc., 2003.

Klimo, John. *Channeling: Investigations on Receiving Information from Paranormal Sources.* Los Angeles: Jeremy P. Tarcher, Inc., 1987.

Marshall, Edward. "Thomas Alva Edison." *The Columbian Magazine,* 3, no. 4 (January 1911).

Peschel, Lisa. *A Practical Guide to The Runes.* St. Paul, Minn.: Llewellyn Publications, 2001.

Roberts, Kenneth. *Henry Gross and His Dowsing Rod.* Garden City, N.Y.: Doubleday & Company, Inc., 1951.

Runes, Dagobert D., ed. *The Diary and Sundry Observations of Thomas Alva Edison.* New York: Philosophical Library, 1948.

Thorsson, Edred. *Runecaster's Handbook: The Well of Wyrd.* York Beach, Maine: Samuel Weiser, Inc., 1988.

Wands, Jeffrey A., with Tom Philbin. *The Psychic in You: Understand Your Natural Psychic Power.* New York: Atria Books, 2004.

Weisberg, Barbara. *Talking to the Dead: Kate and Maggie Fox and the Rise of Spiritualism.* San Francisco: HarperSanFrancisco, 2004.

Winer, Richard and Nancy Osborn. *Haunted Houses.* New York: Bantam, 1979.

Wright, Theon. *The Open Door: A Case History of Automatic Writing.* New York: The John Day Company, 1970.

Internet Resources

Christ Unlimited Ministries. "Bible.com online world," http://www.bible.com (accessed September 15, 2004).

Faulkner, William. The Sound and the Fury. First published 1929. Hypertext edition, ed. Stoicheff, Muri, Deshaye, et al. Saskatoon, Saskatchewan, Canada: U of Saskatchewan, updated Mar. 2003. http://www.usask.ca/english/faulkner (accessed December 5, 2004).

Hurst, Michael J. "Collected Fragments of Tarot History," 1534 France entry, http://www.geocities.com/cartedatrionfi/Fragments/1480-1539.html (accessed August 8, 2004).

Jürgenson, Friedrich. *Sprechfunk mit Verstorbenen: Praktische Kontaktherstellung mit dem Jenseits.* München: Goldmann Verlag, 1981. Online translation "Voice Transmissions With the Deceased," trans. Tom Wingert and George Wynne. http://www.worlditc.org/c_06_juerg_intro.htm (accessed October 10, 2004).

Museum of Talking Boards. "Gallery of Talking Boards: Planchettes," http://www.museumoftalkingboards.com/planchet.html (accessed July 22, 2004).

Index

A

AA-EVP (American Association of Electronic Voice Phenomena), 116-119
Aberasturia, Roberto, 28-29
afferent nerves, 111
After We Die, What Then?, 134
Aladdin, 172
alchemy, 42
American Society of Dowsers, 190, 193, 194, 201, 210
American Theosophical Society, 99
aperture, 68
apparition, 75
Aquinas, Thomas, 237
Ark of the Covenant, 169-170
artwork, tarot, 51-54
automatic writing, 215-235

B

Baldur, 153
Balph, Amanda Bayne, 135
Belanger, Dr. Susan, 80-82
Bell, Alexander Graham, 132
Bhodsvatan, Tatiacha, 225-228
Bible, 191
Bird, Christopher, 192
Bittrich, Dietmar, 50
black mirror, 177-179
Blatty, William Peter, 22-23
Blum, Ralph, J., 162, 157

Bogoras, Walderman, 114
Bond, Elijah J., 18-20
Book of Runes, 152, 157
Bowie, Col. Washington, 18-20
Broca, 101-102
bronze, 168
Bronze Age, 168
Bullshit, 24-25
burial, ritual and, 9
Butler, Lisa, 116-121
Butler, Tom, 116-121

C

Calotype camera, 65
cameras, 68-70, 88
Campbell, Joseph, 238
carte da trionfi, 41
cartomancy, 41, 52
casting of lots, 156
Catholic Church, 170
CCD, 16
Cocciold, Mike, 27-28
Columbian Magazine, The, 99
copper, 168
Court de Gebelin, Antoine, 41
Coven 13, 30-31
Crookes Tube, 96
Crookes, Sir William, 96-97
Cryptique board, 23-24, 31-36
crystal ball, 172-173, 175, 238
Crystal Gazing, 171-172

D

D'Argonell, Oscar, 132
D'Este family, 40
Daguerre, Louis-Jacque-Mande, 64-65
Daguerreotype camera, 64, 73
Day, Christian, 24-26
De Mellet, Louis-Raphael-Lucrece, 41
DeCaro, Jim, 75-78, 174
DeVack, Kyle, 84
Diary and Sundry Observations of
    Thomas Alva Edison, The, 100, 103
Digital Photography Bible, The, 68
Digital Photography, 68
divination, water, 200-201
Divining Hand, The, 192
divining, 188
Donaldson, Terry, 50
double-blind test, 196
dowsing, 187-212, 238
    pendulum, 205-210
    tools for, 189-190
Dowsing, 198
dream, waking, 180
drugs, hallucinogenic, 182

E

ectoplasm, 74
Edison, Minda Miller, 95
Edison, Thomas, 93-105, 112-113, 131
Edison: A Life of Invention, 97
efferent nerves, 111
Egyptians, ancient, 9
Elder Futhark, 152
Electric Mystifying Oracle, 21
electromagnetic spectrum, 67, 132
electronic communication, 95
EMF meter, 210, 212
Encyclopedia of Tarot, 50
Estep, Sarah, 116, 123
etheric force, 98
Everyday Tarot Magic, 48, 49
EVP (Electronic Voice Phenomena),
    109-127, 131-132

EVP Classifications, 123
Exorcist, The, 22-23

F

Fachwerk, 159
Faulkner, William, 217
First Council of Constantinople, 170
Fisk, Danielle, 83
Fitzgerald, Mike, 50
Five Books of Gargantua and
    Pantagruel, The, 41
force, etheric, 98
fortune telling, 41, 169
Fowler, Edward, 216
Fox, Dr. Lawrence K., 67-68, 180-181
Fox, John, 10-11
Fox, Kate, 10-11, 216
Fox, Margaret, 10-11
Fox, Margaretta, 10-11
Fuld, Isaac, 20
Fuld, Kathy, 17, 20-21
Fuld, Stuart, 17, 20-21
Fuld, William, 18-20
Fuller, J.G., 133
Futhark Runes, 160-163

G

Gettysburg, 74, 78-79, 82
Ghost Encounters, 234
Ghost of 29 Megacycles, The, 133
Gillet, Francis A., 85
Gotcher, Dave, 57-58
Gotcher, Holly, 54-57
Gramophone, 113
Graveyard, 76-77
Gutowski, Ace, 188

H

hallucination, 181-182
    hypnagogic, 182
    hypnopompic, 180, 182

hallucinogenic drugs, 182
Hanna, Nicole, 220-225
Hanson-Roberts, Mary, 48
Harden, Thomas, 134
Harsch, Jules, 136
Harsch-Fischbach, Maggy, 136
Hastings, Arthur, 175
Haunted Houses, 104
Havamal, 154-155
Helfrich, Sharon, 135
hieroglyphs, 151
Holy Grail, 199
Horhain, Sungkom, 50
Houck, Margaret, 141-142
How to Do Automatic Writing, 217
Hutchings, William H., 65-66
Hydesville, 10
hypnagogic hallucination, 182
hypnopompic hallucination, 180, 182

I

INIT (International Network for
    Instrumental Transcommunication),
    135, 139, 140
Israel, Paul, 97, 99
ITC (Instrumental
    Transcommunication), 105, 109,
    131-148

J

James Randi Educational Foundation,
    195-196
James, Peter, 234-235
Johnson, Cathy, 84
Johnson, Dr. Craig W., 110-111
Judd, Maggie, 30
Jurgenson, Friedrich, 114-116

K

Kabbalah, 42, 199
Kaplan, Stuart R., 49-50

Kennard Novelty Company, 18-20
Kennard, Charles, 18-20
Kirby and Company, 230-231
Kolek, Ron, 210
Korn, Joey, 198-199, 201-204

L

Laird, Andrew, 88
lens flare, 71
Life After Life, 170
Lincoln, Mary Todd, 66
Literacy, 215-216
Locke, John, 192
logic, 105, 237
lots, casting, 156
L-rods, 189, 194, 201-204
Luminator, 138
Lytle, Dennis, 76-87, 145-147

M

Machell, Ray, 190-191, 193-195,
    204-205
Macy, Mark, 135-148
Matoff, Zoe, 43-48
Matrix, The, 144
McCoy, Edain, 217-220
meditation, 137
Meek, George W., 132-134, 136, 137
Meek, Jeannette, 137
mesmerism, 96
Midgard, 153
Milburn, Ken, 68-74
Miracles in the Storm, 135
mirror gazing, 167-183
mirror, black, 177-179
mist, 74
Moody, Dr. Raymond, 170-176
Morrison, Dorothy, 48-49
Moses, 191-192, 200-201
Mueller, Dr. George Jeffries, 133
Mumler, William H., 66-67, 73
Myths to Live By, 238

N

nerves, types of, 111
New England Ghost Project, 210-212
New York Circle, 216
New York Herald, 98
New York Tribune, 18, 216
Newton, Isaac, 64
Niepce, Joseph Nicephore, 64
Nietzsche, Fredrich, 183
Noleby, stone of, 154
Nostradamus, 176

O

Occam's razor, 89
Ockham, William of, 89
Od, 96
Odin, 96, 151-152, 153-154
Olcott, Henry, 99
Old Diary Leaves, 99
Old Testament, 26-27
Omega: Journal of Death and Dying, 175
Oracle at Delphi, 168-169
orbs, 72-74
Order of the Golden Dawn, The, 42
Oriole board, 20
Osborn, Nancy, 104
ossicles, 110
Osuch, Rev. Dean, 26-27
Ouija board, 15-36, 205, 230
Ouija Novelty Company, 19
Ouijastitions, 22-23

P

pattern recognition, 147
pendulum dowsing, 205-210
pendulum, 190, 204-210
Penn and Teller, 24-25
phonograph, 112-113
photo receptors, 68
photography, spirit, 63-89
planchette, 17, 230

Planchette: The Mystic of Mystics, 231
Poirier, Shawn, 30-31, 32-36
Pollack, Rachel, 43-48
Pracowink, Peter, 50
proof, 12, 105, 148
Psychic in You, The, 174
psychomanteum chamber, 173-175
Pythia, 168

Q

Qwerty board, 27

R

Rabeleis, Francois, 41
Randi, James, 195-197
Raudive, Konstantin, 141
recognition, pattern, 147
Reese, Bert, 99-100
reflection, 167-168
Reginkunnigar, 154
Reichenbach, Baron Karl von, 96, 99
Resonance Working Group, 139-140
Richards, Patrick, 138
Rider-Waite Tarot, 42-43, 50, 53-54, 60
Rivers, Anna, 120
Rivers, Jonathan, 120
Rorschach test, 81-82
Rorschach, Hermann, 81
Rune Gild, 159
Runecaster's Handbook, 152, 159
runes, 151-163, 238
Rusk, Harry Welles, 18-20
Russell, Laurence J., 95, 100-101

S

Salem, 15-17
Salem Witch trials, 15, 192
Schulze, Johann Heinrich, 64
science, spirituality and, 105
Scripture, 26-27, 51-52, 191-192

September 11th, 80
78 Degrees of Wisdom, 43
Sevigny, Paul, 194
Sightings, 234
slate writing, 231-232
Sloane, Madeline, 95-96, 100
Smith, Pamela Colman, 42
solitude, 152
Sound and the Fury, The, 217
sound, 110
spectrum, electromagnetic, 67
speech, 111-112
Spiricom, 133
spirit
    board, 15-36, *see talking board*
    communication, Edison and, 102
    photography, 63-89
    writing, 231
Spiritual Telegraph, 65
spirituality, science and, 105
stochastic resonance, 117
streak, 74
stream-of-consciousness writing, 216-217
Summa Theologica, 237
Sutphen, Dick, 217-218, 226, 229-230
Sutphen, Tara, 218-219, 226, 229, 230
synapses, 111
Szalay, Attila von, 114

T

Talbot, William Henry, 65
talking boards, 15-36, 205, 215, 219, 230
Talking to the Dead, 216
Talmud, 169, 170
tarot, 154, 238
    artwork, 51-54
    cards, 39-60
    language of, 60
telegraph, 95
Tenney Gate House, 211
Tenney, Charles H., 211
test, double-blind, 196

Thorssen, Edred, 152-155, 159
3-D, 181
Timestream Spirit Group, 140, 141
Tolkien, J.R.R., 50
Tree of Life, 199
Tree of the World, 151

U

Urin V'tumin, 169
US Games Systems, Inc., 49-50

V

valve apparatus, 103-104
Vertical Plane, The, 134
vibrator magnet, 97
video ITC, 143
Voice Transmission with the Deceased, 115
voice, 111-112
Voices from Beyond the Telephone, 132
Voices of Eternity, 116
Volo board, 20
vortex, 74

W

Waite, Dr. Arthur Edward, 42
waking dream, 180
Waldherr, Kris, 52-54
Wands, Jeffrey, 174-175
Warren, Ed, 76-77
Warren, Lorraine, 76-77
water,
    divination and, 200-201
    dowsing and, 188, 193-195
Webster, Ken, 134
Wells, Charlotte Fowler, 216
Welsberg, Barbara, 216
Wendt, Denise, 83
Whimsical Tarot, 48
White Lady, 76-77

White Noise, 120
William James Center for
    Consciousness Studies Institute of
    Transpersonal Psychology, 175
Winer, Richard, 104
Winkler, Rabbi Gershon, 169-170,
    199-200
Witch board, 15-36
Witch trials of 1692, 15, 192
Witching, 188
Wood, Maureen, 210-212
World ITC Association, 133, 135, 139
World's Most Haunted Places, The, 135

Wright, J. Gilbert, 104
writing,
    slate, 231-232
    spirit, 231
    stream-of-consciousness, 216-217

Y

Ygdrasil, 151
Young, J. W., 188
Y-rods, 189

About the Author

Jeff Belanger has been studying and writing about the supernatural since 1997. In 1999, Belanger launched Ghostvillage.com as a repository for his writings on the subject. Since then, the site has grown to become the largest paranormal community on the Web, attracting hundreds of thousands of visitors per year.

In his first book, *The World's Most Haunted Places*, Belanger investigated ghostly legends from some of the most supernaturally active locales around the globe. *Communicating With the Dead* delves deeper into understanding human spirituality and the profound nature of spirit contact. Belanger is a regular guest on many regional and national radio programs, is a sought-after lecturer on ghosts and the supernatural, and has been featured on television programs about the paranormal. He currently haunts Bellingham, Massachusetts, with his wife, Megan.

Also by Jeff Belanger:

6 x 9, 256 pp.
ISBN: 1-56414-764-9, $15.99
30 B & W Photos

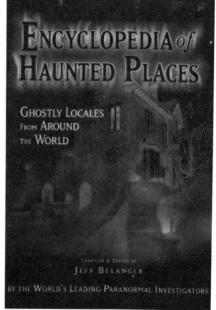

7 x 10, 360 pp.
ISBN: 1-56414-799-1, $19.99
More than 100 B & W Photos